Stepping Stones

Stepping Stones

ISABELLA WALLACE

BALBOA.
PRESS

A DIVISION OF HAY HOUSE

Balboa Press books may be ordered through booksellers or by contacting:

Balboa Press
A Division of Hay House
1663 Liberty Drive
Bloomington, IN 47403
www.balboapress.com
1-(877) 407-4847

Because of the dynamic nature of the Internet, any web addresses or links contained in this book may have changed since publication and may no longer be valid. The views expressed in this work are solely those of the author and do not necessarily reflect the views of the publisher, and the publisher hereby disclaims any responsibility for them.

The author of this book does not dispense medical advice or prescribe the use of any technique as a form of treatment for physical, emotional, or medical problems without the advice of a physician, either directly or indirectly. The intent of the author is only to offer information of a general nature to help you in your quest for emotional and spiritual well-being. In the event you use any of the information in this book for yourself, which is your constitutional right, the author and the publisher assume no responsibility for your actions.

Certain stock imagery © Thinkstock.
Any people depicted in stock imagery provided by Thinkstock are models, and such images are being used for illustrative purposes only.

Printed in the United States of America

ISBN: 978-1-4525-6565-1 (sc)
ISBN: 978-1-4525-6566-8 (e)

Balboa Press rev. date: 12/20/2012

"This book is dedicated to my beautiful mum, the bravest person I will ever know, when I see you again I am going to give you a huge hug"

table of contents

1

the early years

Blinking my mum opened her eyes, waking up in the recovery room of the local hospital after just having an emergency caesarean section with her third child after a placenta abruption. In those days expectant mothers were given a full anaesthetic for a caesarean section and the dads were left to worry and to pace the corridors until the baby was born. 'Where are my teeth', mum asked the nurse who was checking that she was ok after noticing that her patient had woken up. I imagine that the nurse thought her patient was going to be sick as she had here hand over her mouth. Charming, never mind your lovely healthy new baby, just remember about your teeth Mum! Poor mum, she never did live this one down. My mum lost all of her teeth at the age of just twenty-one when she was pregnant with my older brother, nobody but the dentist saw her without them, not even my dad. She NEVER took them out anytime but to clean them, with the bathroom door locked!

I always loved pink and sparkly things, a real girly girl who loved to sing and dance, dress up in my mum's shoes and wearing her real black rabbit fur coat, playing pretend mummies with my dolls, in reality I was a princess; the youngest child of three.

My appearance was not a happy occasion for my older siblings though, my darling brother, Andrew, six years old and my sister Lyndsay, who was four years old at the time of my birth, wanted a baby brother and thought it would be best if I went in to the rubbish bin. Andrew and Lyndsay always used to me that I was found at the side of the road in a cardboard box and that the family felt sorry for me, so they adopted me. My dad used to jokingly say when he was asked if he had a family, that he had one of each; a boy, a girl and me. It is a good job I have a sense of humour or I would have been wearing my jacket buttoned up at the back and swaying in the corner, requiring unlimited intense psychiatric therapy. Fortunately for me my parents did not want to put me in the rubbish bin, so I was taken home and spoiled rotten, just like my brother and sister!

My parents were married when my mum was only nineteen; she was thinner than thin, had long brown wavy hair, that she used to iron straight before going on nights out, this was before hair straighteners had been invented. She would lay her long hair on the ironing board, put brown paper on top of it and then iron it. During the nights out dancing, her hair would start to get wavy as the night wore on. On her wedding day she had her hair up and she looked gorgeous in her white lace wedding dress. My dad had his twenty first birthday the day after their wedding; he was a Beatles looky likey, same hair cut and build as John Lennon in his wedding suit. I have some of their wedding photos; they looked so young but a very very happy couple. My mum's cousin was her bridesmaid, she wore a slim fitting long gold dress, mums younger sister was only about five years old at the time and she threw a massive tantrum until she got a white lace dress too. She looked like a little doll in her dress, with her little gloves, white shoes and her frilly ankle socks. My parents honeymooned in Callander, Scotland, mum thought that she was abroad as she had not been out the area before. The hotel room they had booked shared a bathroom at the end of the hall with the other rooms, I cannot even imagine having to get up to use the bathroom in the middle of the night and having to walk along a corridor in my pyjamas; never mind being a young couple on their honeymoon and sharing a bathroom with the other guests. That was just how hotels were in those days though. Mum told me that there was a scary old woman who sat on the landing in her rocking chair, knitting all the time. My mum insisted that they went out every day to sight see as she did not want the hotel staff to talk about the newly weds staying in their room all day! Mum and dad settled into married life in their small apartment with their one bedroom room and lounge/kitchen, dad worked as a mechanic during the week and worked as a baker's agent on a bakery van during the evenings and at the weekends, mum worked full time as a secretary within the local police station.

Her granny lived next door to the police station and she used to come around to my mum's office with something for her to eat, she would tell the sergeant that mum was entitled to a break. She was the type of woman that you did not argue with! My mum's career came to an end when she left her secretarial post as she took her maternity leave in preparation for giving birth to my brother in the local hospital. My parents had been married for two years when my brother arrived, chubby, dark hair and blue eyes; he was a mixture of them both. Mum felt able to come home straight after the birth but in those days you had no choice but to stay in the hospital for a full week after having giving birth to your first child. When her father in law came to collect her and my brother she had to drive the car back home as my granda was a nervous driver and he just handed her the car keys the minute she came out of the hospital ward. My brother was the first grandchild for both sides of the family, I imagine that my mum's parents were especially taken with their new grandson as they had two daughters of their own; a fourteen year age gap between their daughters and they sadly lost a baby girl in between, my dad's parents had two sons after many years of trying and unfortunately losing many babies. Medical care for pregnant women in my grandparents time was not as good as it is nowadays, even in my mums time she did not have as much in the way of anti natal care; as women do now, she never had a baby scan or frequently went to see the midwife or health visitor. In those days when women started their families they did not go back to work after the baby was born, this was the beginning of my mum becoming a housewife and mummy, a role that she really enjoyed but I am sure she would have enjoyed going back to work for a rest sometimes. When Andrew was a few months old the bedroom ceiling in my mum and dad's apartment down on top of their bed, it was lucky that nobody was hurt and that Andrew slept in his cot at mum's side of the bed. This was when they decided that it would be for the best if they moved to a two bedroom family house as mum had plans to have four children.

Their second child, a baby girl was born at home, in their new bungalow when Andrew was two years old. My dad asked mum if she was 'going to be long' as he was worried about taking time off work. I can only imagine the look she gave him. She told him just to go to work. Dad's did not take as much of a role during the labour and birth of their children as they do now, my dad was at work when my sister was born and did not know that he had a new baby daughter until he arrived home from work that evening, Lyndsay was born on my dad's birthday. Both granny's were at my mum's side during the birth as was my brother, my paternal granny rushed out of the house taking my brother by the hand when Lyndsay was born as she had her eyes wide open, this gave my granny a huge fright.

My sister was and still is the image of my mum, brown curly hair, glasses and slim, it is uncanny at times looking at photos of mum when she was younger as Lyndsay is her spitting image. Baby number three (me) came along unexpectedly six weeks early when Lyndsay was four years old; mum was rushed into hospital for an emergency caesarean when she started bleeding. Both mother and baby thrived but my mum was really disappointed, as she wanted to give birth at home again, not having to endure an operation in a sterile hospital environment, she wanted the family around her as she had the time before. My dad was advised to have 'the op', a vasectomy; as it was not a good idea for mum to have the fourth baby that she had really wanted to complete her family. Dad did what was best for his wife.

The nurses loved it when my dad visited mum and I as he brought them cream cakes from his baker's van. This was his full time job by then, swapping a dirty mechanic's job for a baker's agent in a pure white overall. I was born with blonde hair, blue/green eyes and probably looked more like my dad's side of the family; I certainly have my dad's cheeky face, nature and gift of the gab. We could both be Olympic gold medallist for talking. We all had a very good childhood, I am not saying that it was perfect as there is no such thing but it worked and we were all happy.

Dad was and still is a softy, mum was the disciplinarian, however; we did not ever take advantage of our parents and as a good friend often tells me 'there is a huge difference between spoiled and spoilt'. We had respect and showed respect for the adults in our lives, still do and it is a pity that the kids of this generation do not.

I was taken back to the first family home when I was a mere two weeks old, the two-bedroom bungalow in a street of around ten houses. When my parent had been married for 3 years they bought this house; the total market price was £3750, mum and dad paid a deposit of £750 and this made their mortgage £42 per month. An extension was put on to the back of the house six years after they first moved in after they extended their family, giving them another bedroom and a dining room, therefore giving my parents a larger bedroom. Andrew then had his own bedroom, with a skylight window, which I thought was so cool, he also had a small black and white television in his room where I would spend many hours watching the kid's programmes and I would try not to be tempted to poke at his goldfish or to use the tools on his workbench. Many times temptation went out of the window! Lyndsay and I shared the other bedroom, we had bunk beds, and Lyndsay always slept on the top bunk, because she was the eldest.

At night when the bunk beds were separated my sister and I would jump from one bunk bed to the other pretending that we were on ships that were sinking as we rescued each other. That was until mum came through to tell us to get to sleep, we could hear her coming through to our bedroom from the lounge and we would lie down and pretend to be asleep but she knew we were pretending, we could not get anything past her. We knew how far we could push mum, she had a look that we knew said 'that is enough now', where dad never said no to us. Mum did all the decorating in the house, painting, wallpapering and tiling, usually through the night when we were asleep or when we stayed at our grandparents, her dad taught her how to do it and she taught me when I got my first house. When Lyndsay and I got a bit older, mum decorated our bedroom in The Muppets wallpaper; a television programme we loved to watch every Saturday night starring Jim Henson's Muppets. The spare roll of the wallpaper was given to us kids to play with. We made a theatre and play, cutting out the characters, sticking them onto lolly sticks and using an old cardboard box as the theatre, our small torches were the theatre lights. Mum watched us recreate the Muppet Show many times; she never once said that she had had enough of watching us playing.

I remember one Christmas mum had made me some dolls bed covers using her sewing machine for the cradle that Santa had brought me and she had also made one of my old dresses fit my dolly. I played with them for hours, dressing and undressing my doll and putting her to bed. Lyndsay got a Casio keyboard and Andrew received a chemistry set that year, he spent the whole day with the goggles on and he had red marks on his face when mum eventually got him to take them off when it was time for bed. I took a brilliant Polaroid picture of Andrew with his goggles on top of his head and his hair sticking up, standing behind my paternal granda. Lyndsay was always pushed through the living room door first by Andrew and I, just to see if Santa had been and was gone, because she was the bravest out of us all. That year I also got a small pink toy piano, I remember it really clearly because there was a toy monkey sitting on the small stool. We all watched Poseidon and The Towering Inferno in our pyjamas that Christmas night after both sets of grandparents and my auntie went home, even now we have our Christmas days together as a family, my poor mum having to cook a meal for us all. At the start of their married life, before they had their kids mum and dad went to one set of parents one year for Christmas dinner and the other set of parents the next, when their three little angels came along it was probably easier for the grandparents to come to our house to have Christmas dinner.

They loved watching us open and play with our new toys; we would all get dressed up in our best clothes, my dad, granda's and brother with their shirt and ties on and mum, granny's, my auntie and myself with our dresses or skirts on, Lyndsay preferred trousers. We would have our dinner and afterwards the adults would watch the television or they would join in with us while we played with our new board games. Sometimes my dads brother Robert would come over later on in the evening with his son who was born on Christmas day when I was four. He is the only cousin that we have. My mum's dad liked to drink whiskey neat but he would get very stern looks from his wife, my granny if he had too many. Christmas night often ended in mum playing the piano and both of my granda's singing. Mum would also get her record player out and put on some of her old vinyl 45 records.

One year Andrew and Lyndsay received a motorbike, a scrambler 50cc; to share for their Christmas, they woke my mum and dad up by starting it up and revving it in the kitchen. The smell was awful and there were exhaust fumes throughout the house. They ended up falling out about having to share it so dad bought Lyndsay one of her own, they then spent many hours riding on it around the fields nearby our house, that was until Andrew got bored and curious, he took his motorbike to pieces but he soon found out that his attempt to put it back together again failed.

Dad had to arrange for a local motorbike dealer to collect the pieces in a trailer so that it could be rebuilt and then sold. This started the motorbike phase that Andrew and Lyndsay went through; they had the leather jackets, leather gloves and motorbike helmets. I stayed out of the way with my dolls usually but sometimes I became brave enough to have a ride on the back of the motorbike.

One out of the two Alsatians that we had at the time was terrified of all males, mum and dad had bought the dog from a woman who's house was filthy and the dog had obviously been ill treated, the first thing mum did was give him a bath, scrubbing him all over, even the insides of his ears were filthy. We called him Rover and he eventually fitted in well with the family and the other dog, Doug. The first Christmas that Rover was with us he got that scared when one of my granda's came in to the house that he ran all around the living room in a panic, trying to hide and ended up knocking the Christmas tree over. It was a shame and not the dog's fault, how people can be cruel to animals I will never know.

Doug died when he was ten years old, he had been unwell for a while but it was still a shock, we had him since he was a puppy and we had all grown up with him. It happened on a Saturday night just as my parents were getting ready to go out for the night; we were staying with our granny and granda as we often did at the weekends. Dad buried him in the back garden as mum cancelled their night out; they were just too upset to go out. Rover was a bit lost after that, being the only dog so in time dad went out and bought my mum a Yorkshire terrier as a surprise, the breeders called him Fritz as he was supposed to be going to a German couple but they had changed their minds. Rover loved having a small friend to play with; in fact he used to squeeze into the smaller dog bed at night and cuddle into Fritz. Scotch was the next dog and then little Sooty came next, both Yorkshire terriers.

There was a bit of sibling rivalry between Lyndsay and I when we were younger and we would fight daily. Sometimes she hit me really hard and made me cry. Our dad would tell me that she had slipped when she really was meaning to cuddle me; it did not make me feel any better. Andrew never did get involved in the fighting, he was the quiet one but I do remember him hitting Lyndsay once, although I cannot remember why but it did make me smile when she was crying for a change.

Once Lyndsay punched me so hard that my tooth pierced the skin just under my lip, I still have the small unattractive scar now, I am sure she just thought of me as her very annoying thumb-sucking little sister. I just loved sucking my thumb, I did it all the time and when one thumb ended up with a suck lump or bright orange after drinking Lucozade I would swap it for the other thumb. I also used to rub labels while I sucked my thumb or I would rub my mum's clothes, even now some materials feel sooky and I can feel my mouth watering, tempting me to put my thumb back in to my mouth. My teeth were not damaged as a result of the years of thumb sucking and I did stop eventually when I was around 14 years old.

As a way of trying to get back at Lyndsay for hitting me daily, I scored her name into the dining table, using a fork. I had hoped for her to get a huge telling off, the only problem was that being a pre schooler at that time I wrote my N's back to front and got caught out. Sugar! Speaking of sugar, I had a nasty accident after climbing up on to the kitchen worktops one day; I was looking for something nice to eat. I had not noticed that I had left the cutlery drawer slightly open and when I jumped down with a biscuit in my hand I ripped my backside on the metal edge of the drawer. God, I can still feel it now! Mum got Lyndsay to make me a cup of strong tea with what tasted like half the sugar bowl in it while she cleaned me up and calmed me down, I do have a large scar now though to remind me, as if I would forget that one. That is what I get for being greedy! My dad says that it is one way of identifying my body if I were ever washed up on the shore. Mum was always the calm one in a crisis; once, Lyndsay woke up during the night as she had been sick, she had went through to the living room to get mum and dad freaked out, he said ' oh my god, someone has broken in and tried to murder her'. Mum explained that she had just been sick and the red stuff on her pyjamas was tomato soup! Mum changed her, cleaned her up, put her back to bed and poured my dad a stiff drink.

We did not see much of our dad during the week as he left the house very early for his job on the bakery van, and arrived home after we were in bed every night. I remember him getting us to help him count up the weekly takings on a Saturday, this was usually after he had taken us to the shops and treated us to sweets, a toy or a comic, sometimes all three. He would lock the back door and empty a cloth bag full of money on to the living room carpet, we each had our separate piles of coins where we would then be given the task of counted them into pounds before bagged them up, ready to be banked. It is one way of helping your child with their mathematics. We also became experts at bagging bread rolls, three kids and two adults in the mornings putting three rolls in a row in the bottom of the paper bag and another three on the top, then turning the top corners of the bag twice. There was a knack to it and sometimes the bags would rip when we turned them, dad would get annoyed, as he had to pay for the bags, when he was not looking mum would swap us for her bag and make the torn bag 'magically disappear' before dad spotted it. Days like that were very happy times spent together as a family, although we probably did not think so back then. When my granny and my auntie came to our house to look after us on the Saturday night's that we were not staying with our other grandparent's, when mum and dad were having a night out, our granny would send us out to the van to get her favourite snowball biscuits. We also had a 'stock' cupboard in the house where we would get our playtime snack for school. It was very handy when a crisp company had a promotion running as we always had enough tokens to get the offer. During the school holidays we would take turns in going to 'help' dad for the day in the van, it felt like we were getting up during the middle of the night. When it was my turn I would fill a bag with goodies during the day, meringues, cakes, biscuits. Not realizing that I was planning to eat my dad's earnings. Dad would put what I had in my bag back on the shelves without me noticing when I was distracted by chatting to the regular customers. I sat on a small white stool that he had in the van, right next to the sink where he would wash his hands when we would stopped in the housing schemes. I am still partial to a meringue or two.

Dad also did the local village gala day bags one year, parents would pay for their kid to have a bag with a sausage roll, cake and juice; a sort of packed lunch for the gala day. That year he was not expecting it to be as busy and he ran out of ready-made bags, we all had to muck in and make up extra bags.

2

primary school

When we were all small and after I started primary school mum helped run the local playgroup, a local group for pre school children where they could socialise and play with other children their own age. Mum was the treasurer as well as taking her turn at being a play leader; a few of her friends were also the play leaders. On the subject of the playgroup, mum recalled how anxious she had been about leaving me when my time came, as I was very quiet and shy, very difficult to believe now! My mum's close friend, Eve told my mum not to worry, to go home and have a cup of tea, as I would be ok. Eve still tells the story of the first time she heard me talk. I pulled at her top and said 'Eve, can I paint? '. I think she nearly had to sit down. I do not think I have stopped talking since that day, my granda used to say it was as if I had been injected with a gramophone needle. I did have a good teacher in Eve as she can talk all day and is doing a good job at teaching her granddaughter to become a little chatterbox.

After a heavy snowfall one year, Andrew and Lyndsay and I asked dad if we could have one of his large breadbaskets to use as a sledge. We spent all day sledging down the short cut hill, which lead to the village, our friends were jealous of our sledge as most of them were using plastic bags that they were wearing like pants as their sledges. A bit bumpy on the backside! They took turns with our 'sledge' when their plastic bags burst. Why does the snow not fall as deeply or as brightly when you are an adult? When we got back to the house to wait for our dinner, Lyndsay and Andrew spent ages building an igloo, taking ages to pack the snow into brick shapes. I was told I was far too little to help so I played with Rover; he loved to jump up in the air to catch the snowballs I had made for him. I remember playing in the igloo and crying when it melted. Rover was also really handy during the summer time when the bees were around, we used to shout on him when we were playing outside and a bee was buzzing around us, he would come running, jump up and eat the bee. We played at chasing with the poor dog around the elephant grass at the front of the house, all of the dogs that we had were so placid, we could chase them and pull at their tails, they were very protective of us.

Dad's dad used to do the garden at the weekend, gardening was one of his hobbies, my own dad was not interested, it was too quiet and slow for him to be interested in plus he did not have any spare time either. My paternal granda was a case and a half, he would lock my dad's van keys inside the van after he had washed it, cleaning the really dirty marks off with a brillo pad or wire wool; he had to take the door off to get back into the van and he would also tell mum that we should not be playing where he had just done the gardening, not because he was a grumpy old man it was just that he was so proud of his gardening skills. Mum let us play in the garden anyway.

Lyndsay had a massive brown rabbit, it was more like a hare and Andrew had a black and white one; I used to take Andrew's rabbit for walks up and down the street in my doll's pram, one day while I took my furry baby for a walk I did not notice that a cow had escaped from the field at the bottom of the street until it started chased me back up my house. I was terrified and mum came rushing out of the house to see what was happening. I still do not like cows! The cow was probably more scared of my screaming than I was of it chasing me. My mum shooed it away and got me into the garden, closing the gate. Just over the fence at the back of our house there was a large hay field where we played with the other kids in the street.

When the farmer had piled up the hay into bales we used to climb up onto them, playing at tag, running from one bale to another before the person who was 'it' caught us. Whoever else was in your team helped you to get back up on top of the bale before you were caught. Personally, I would say that living in that house was the happiest time for our family; it was probably hard work for my mum, having three kids to look after and not seeing much of her husband. It probably was not the best time for my dad either as he was always working and I am sure he missed his wife and his family. My mum always said that she was at her happiest when we had all our friends in the garden playing, she did not mind how noisy we all got or if she had to make dinner for more than her own three children.

I do remember the family parties where dad would wake us up after probably being told not to by our mum, he would sneak us bread sticks then take us through, half asleep in our pyjamas to see the family and friends having fun, dancing, singing, playing games and having a drink. Mum used to pretend that she was really annoyed with him for doing this, but he just wanted to spent time with us as he missed us when he was out working. Mum used to get her 45's out, her favourite record was Bobby's Girl by Marcie Blane. Dad used to do 'the bump' a dance where two people would bump their alternate hip against the others hip, I think that if you did this dance with my dad once you never ever did it again with him as he bumped you that hard he nearly put you through the wall. One of their games involved trying to get peanuts into the glass upturned lampshade by throwing them, mum used to play the piano and I would sing along sometimes if I was not feeling shy. That was the beginning of the 'Von Trapp' party duets; Mum would sing alongside me at the beginning when I felt nervous and then she would just stop and keep playing, leaving me to it. Bugger! Mum was very musical, she played the piano until she was fourteen, and she was one exam away from being able to becoming a piano teacher when she gave it up, she could also play the accordion, the organ and the harpsichord. I think that the good-looking boy a few doors down from her house distracted her!! My dad.

Mum and dad rented a shop in the village square and opened it up as a café/bakers, the walls were bright orange and the seats were brown. My mum ran the shop while dad continued to go out on his bakers van, her auntie Lilly worked during the week, mum's younger sister, Pauline and another girl, Caroline worked there on a Saturday. Little did I know that I would eventually work with Caroline as a nursery nurse and that we would become close friends, strange how things turn out? Myself, Lyndsay and Andrew would go straight there after school, I was not at all happy if all the meringues had been sold before I got in from school.

The overheads were really expensive, the rules and regulations made running a cater establishment very difficult so dad changed jobs during this time, becoming a double-glazing salesman, where he was very successful and mum returned to her role as housewife and mother. Who would have though a quiet man could become a profitable salesman.

Lyndsay had a birthday party one year, im not sure what age she was, maybe eleven or twelve as it was the year before she went to the high school. What I do remember however, was the thunder and lightening storm, the raining lashing down. Andrew, Lyndsay and I sat at the living room window watching the lightening and wondering who would turn up for the party. We did not think anyone would come out in that weather but I think her full class turned up at the house, they had a great time doing the 'pogo' dance, playing kissing games and eating the goodies mum had made. Andrew and his friend Bob were the dj, they probably felt really grown up and cool, and I was just happy having a dress on and dancing. Those were the days when kids were happy with having a party at home, ice cream, sandwiches, homemade cake; receiving socks and sweets for presents. Dad dropped all the party guests off home after the party was over, it must have looked like a carload of monkeys, especially when they were shouting out of the window and giving passers by the finger. Sure was an eye opener for my dad!

The next morning we noticed that the thunderstorm had torn up all the tar on the short cut path where we had played when it snowed, that lead to the village. It had just been tarred and to this day it still remains in the same condition.

Dad woke us for school each morning after he had changed jobs when I was 6; we would get dressed in front of the enclosed coal fire while we ate our toast and drank our tea. Then he would drop us off at school sometimes, giving my mum a long lie. At the weekends we would get up in time to watch the children's television programmes. The Banana Splits and Saturday Swap Shop, we would sit eating our cornflakes in our pyjamas. We did not wake our mum or dad; we just chilled out in front of the television until they got up. I was just about to call the Swap Shop one morning to swap Lyndsay and Andrew for a pair of ice skates but dad came into the sitting room just as I had written down the number to call.

I remember the day when mum was dropping us off for school and as she turned the car to head home the back wheel got stuck in a drain at the kerb, there was nothing that we could do, we just had to go to school while she got help to get her out. Those were the days before mobile phones were invented; we had just recently got a telephone installed in the house. It must have been a nightmare for her. The men from the local garage managed to push her car out of the drain, I bet she went home for a lay down after that.

My hair was long when I first started primary school and I would take my clasps, ribbons and bobbles to mum to do my hair in the mornings, I loved getting my hair brushed and put up in the bobbles and ribbons. In our photographs I have long hair and a really pretty party dress on at Christmas and then the next photograph in the album, which was on my granny's birthday in the February, I have the same dress on; but my hair has been cropped like a boy and I have no front teeth. I still do not like that photo! I think mum got my hair cut as it was very fine and she thought that it would grow in thicker, pity my teeth had fallen out at the same time. Not a very flattering photograph of me though.

3

caravan weekends

I was still a baby in a carrycot when mum and dad bought their first touring caravan. I still wonder now how they could fit three kids, two adults and at one point two large Alsatian dogs, we would go away most weekends so that dad could have a break from his work. The touring caravan was eventually upgraded for a static caravan on sites, which were on the seaside coasts of Scotland. Craigton Park, near St Andrews was to us as Alton Towers Theme Park is to a kid nowadays, they had a model railway, boats on the pond, bands would play on the stage, where I would often sit on the steps singing along and dreaming of going to stage school. We had picnics outside while we listened to the bands or we had meals in the café, the dogs lay underneath the table and slept, it was a proper family fun day out. We would go to the pancake and ice cream shop in St Andrews high street, and when we went to the toyshop we always got a toy. In fact one time when we first entered the toyshop I spotted two small kitten toys and their mum in a basket just at the front door. I must have given dad my pleading 'please daddy' face; he lifted the two kittens and carried them around the shop as we browsed, so that nobody else could have them. The shop assistant panicked when she noticed that the kittens were not in the basket, she thought that they had been stolen and was so relieved when we appeared at the till to buy them, of course we could not buy the kittens without buying their mum too. I was one happy little girl that day.

On Friday's when we got a little older mum would take us back home from visiting our granny's and by the time our dad came home from his work we would be all packed up, washed and in our pyjamas ready to go in to the car on our way to the caravan. We were bundled into sleeping bags in the back of the car and put straight to bed when we arrived, often sound asleep.

It felt like an exciting midnight trip, even although we knew where we were going. Just because we were sitting in our pyjamas and sleeping bags in the back seat of the car, travelling in the dark, it just felt thrilling. When the caravan season had closed during the winter months we still visited our grandparents on Fridays, we would come home, get washed, the three of us in the one bath and then we would get into our pyjamas so that we could watch The Walton's and It's a Knockout on the television with mum. If we were good we were allowed to stay up until our dad came home from his work. We visited our maternal granny, granda and auntie every Monday, Wednesday and Friday evenings, granny would feed a whole packet of chocolate digestives to the dogs and mum would eventually, when I had grown up a little bit more, allow me to go across the road to visit my other granny and granda. Every Friday meant grocery shopping with my granny and auntie; mum had a yellow shopping bag and my granny's was purple. Those horrible bags are stuck in my memory bank; plastic bags were not used much back then. My granny sometimes bought me real baby clothes for my baby doll out of Woolworth's, I would always be allowed to pick something as a treat, it was part of the Friday shopping, I usually asked for something very girly, like a little pink dress for my baby doll or a small dolls tea set.

You did not give that granny any cheek because she had a talent, she could get her slipper off of her foot, smack your backside and have it back on her foot before you even felt the sting, it was just like a boomerang, or a cowboy with his gun.

One weekend when we were at the caravan site, dad arrived back from the shops with the usual newspapers, crisps, sweets and milk etc, as he did every Saturday but he handed me a paper bag. It contained a rag doll! I was still such a girly girl and just loved my dolls, she had long brown wool hair and a long purple flowery dress, and I loved her to bits. I named her Jemima from the television programme Playschool; I took her everywhere with me, she sits beside my bed now but she is not as pretty as she once was, it did not help that Lyndsay stamped on her face with her dirty shoes on!!!

We went to look at cars once with mum and dad, I do not remember where; all I do remember is that the owners of the garage had a giant black poodle dog, it scared me. It was the size of a horse. I could not believe it when I discovered that I had left Jemima at the garage, we were too far away to turn back to collect her, I was in tears, devastated and it did not help that Andrew and Lyndsay were filling my head with thoughts of the giant poodle eating my favourite dolly.

How the dog would be tossing her in to the air and shaking her stuffing out. Thinking about it now, they probably hid her from me when we were leaving the garage. Dad called the garage when we got home and the owners promised to post my doll back to me, when she finally arrived I could not believe that they had bent her legs up her back when they parcelled her up. I did not want to go to school that day, all I wanted to do was stay at home and cuddle Jemima all day, I was so relieve that she had survived that giant monster dog and also being posted back to me. My uncle Robert also used to torment me by putting Jemima in my granny's fridge or up on her lampshade, I would be so upset if I could not find her. My granny would tell my uncle off and ask him to stop making me cry but the next thing I knew he had hidden Jemima from me again. Lyndsay had a stuffed toy Scotty dog that she called Mac, she also still has him now; she was not as attached to him as I was with Jemima but she was really unhappy when Andrew hid him on top of the caravan roof one weekend, it gave Jemima a rest for a change.

Elie caravan site was just beside the beach, my brother was addicted to flying kites and you were honoured if he let you have a turn but god help you if you let it come down. When he was not flying his kite he was collecting spent bullets on and around the beach and I would go with him too as I loved the small bunkers, imagining they were houses and playing near him in the small pools, squashing the sand between my toes or jumping the waves. I suppose he was told to look out for me by our parents, Lyndsay did not come with us very often she was more interested in doing cartwheels, standing on her head or playing football in those days but she did come to my rescue one day as we walked back to the caravan after being on the beach exploring. We did not have our shoes on as we had been paddling in the sea, I stood on a bee that was laying on the grass, the bee's sting stuck in my foot and unfortunately for Lyndsay I could not put my weight on my foot. Speaking of my weight, I was a very plump child and Lyndsay was really skinny but she still managed to carry me all the way back to the caravan, I think mum and dad must have thought I was being murdered when they heard me roaring, but the only thing that had been murdered was the bee. We stayed at Elie for many years; Andrew eventually stopped going when he was old enough to stay at home by himself and when it was not seen as cool to go away for the weekends with his parents and his younger sisters. So when Lyndsay also wanted to stop going, my parents decided that it was time to move to another site.

Lochearnhead caravan site was the next weekend base for the family; it meant that the whole family could enjoy the Loch when dad bought a speedboat. Encouraged by Andrew and Lyndsay, who had become interested in family weekends away again as soon as the speedboat was brought in to the conversations. My dad has always been scared of water so it was a strange thing for him to buy but he ended up having lots of fun; I think he overcome his fear of the water. We were all kitted out with wellies, life jackets etc. My dad even bought a 'captains' hat and a jacket that made him look just like 'Captain Birds Eye'. It was so funny. Being a novice, dad asked the local yachting club's captain to show him and the family the ropes when we all went for our first weekend with the speedboat. I can still remember the terrified look on dad's face when mum slammed on the breaks of the Land Cruiser after reversing the trailer and speedboat with my dad in, into the Loch as instructed by the yachting club expert. By doing this quickly it meant that the boat would slide smoothly straight off of the trailer, launching it for the first time. Kind of a 'You've Been Framed' moment! Dad just was not expecting it to happen. My dad got used to launching the boat with time, mum did not even blink if she was the one in the speedboat during the launch, dad being behind the wheel of the car and in fact Lyndsay used to drive the Land Cruiser and launch the boat even before she was age to drive. We did not get in to water-skiing but we did get a skibob, a sort of bullet shaped inflatable which was towed behind the boat, needless to say dad did not take his turn on it, mum did though and ended up in the water. I was as adventurous as my dad and did not try the skibob but I did swim in the Loch, 'once' with Lyndsay and it was more than freezing, plus I had seen too many horror films and watched too many Twilight Zone episodes; I kept waiting for something to grab my ankle. Dad eventually sold that speedboat and bought a faster one that the whole family also enjoyed using, even my grandparents. Us kids being kids stopped going for weekends away at Lochearnhead and spent time at home instead. Mum and dad sold the boat, jetty, the caravan and moved to a two-bedroom cabin on the same site but up on the hill at the end of the site where it was peaceful and quiet. Many a year they have spent relaxing at the cabin, where my dad has no access to a phone so he is completely away from his work as a salesman.

My dad's uncle, his daughter, her husband and their 2 boys came up from Yorkshire to stay at Loch Earn for a short holiday; they also had fun using the speedboat. My cousins and I were in our very early teens; we went exploring and found a dead fish floating in a small shallow pool. We talked my mum into giving us a sharp knife; and we gave the fish a post mortem, got my mum to film it on the video camera. The close ups were pretty gruesome, I remember holding the tongue up to the camera on the end of the knife. Im surprised that nobody was sick, although my younger cousin Bob pretended for the camera. Being the oldest I was in charge of the knife, of course but I let David, Bob's older brother take his turn.

There was not much left of that poor fish after we had finished. I think my dad still has that video tape somewhere. We were word perfect on 'The Chicken' song from the programme Spitting Image, we also acted out the diet coke advert and the stranger danger advert, 'Charlie and I were in the park', our poor parent having to listen to that for a full weekend. Maybe the alcohol helped them to blank it all out!

4

having fun with our grandparents

When the Atari console game first came on to the market Andrew got one, he would play at tennis on it daily. Well I say tennis but it looked more like lines, the 'court' was the television screen with a white line through the middle of it, dividing the court, the tennis 'players' moved in a straight line only; up and down at the side of the screen and the square 'ball' bounced between them. Andrew played it a lot on his own black and white small-screened television at home but when he took it out to our paternal grandparents house to play on their larger television, my granny was worried that the 'ball' would scratch her television screen with it constantly going backwards and forwards. Andrew was only allowed to play it a few times, as our granny was uneasy about her television. I think she was concerned as this was something new to her, and she did not understand that the game was behind the glass screen.

When more games came on to the market for this console our mum got addicted to Pac Man, she would play it for hours. When we got home from school, the mains plug for the Atari was red hot, too hot to touch or remove from the socket. It was so funny for us as kids to watch our mum get so animated over a computer game designed for children.

My granny's brothers enlisted in the armed forces during the war and when the war ended they settled down in various areas of England where they met and married their wives and had families of their own. They visited my granny as often as they could and my dad would take my granny down to visit them too. One of her brothers would turn up for a weekend with a small red suitcase, just like the Chancellor of the Exchequer's, all he brought with him were old photographs, there was never a change of clothes or a toothbrush in that red case. This brother also drove up to Scotland from London with his wife, she had sat for the entire journey with her jacket caught in the door; half bent over for around 5 hours, it could not have been a comfortable trip for her.

Lyndsay had taken her huge rabbit out to visit our granny's house; granny was also enjoying a visit from her brother who lived in Yorkshire at the time. Instead of keeping the rabbit in the garden (granda would not allow her to anyway) Lyndsay brought it in to the house, the rabbit was doing the toilet in the lounge and ended up chewing straight through my granny's telephone cable. My dad's uncle fixed the cable for his sister but he could not stop laughing, he had tears streaming down his face while he fixed the telephone as my granda was cursing and chasing the rabbit around the lounge to try and catch it. He wanted it back it its cage, he was worried about it getting out and in to his precious garden to eat his prize roses.

My granny, dad's mum, had to have both of her knees replaced due to her arthritis when I was about nine and she had a really long stay in hospital, because they did one knee at a time. Maybe me sitting on her knee all the time did not help, in every photo there I am plonked on her knee. I did mention that I was a chubby child? My granda let me away with murder when I visited him when granny was in the hospital, we would watch Blue Peter then he would empty the cornflakes box so that we could attempt to re-create whatever they were making on that day during the programme. He taught me how to tie my shoelaces and how to play draughts on a board that his father in law had made out of a fruit crate; the black and red counters were also hand made and looked as good as any shop bought set, probably better. That was great fun until I could beat him at the game!

He also let me take all of the cushions off of the sofa and pile them at the end of the living room where I would run and jump on top of them. My mum made his daily meals and would clean the entire house on a Saturday for him when granny was still in the hospital, the only thing that she minding doing was emptying the jar that he kept at the side of his chair. It was an old jam jar that he had painted black, he used it to spit in after he had been smoking his pipe and also to put his spent matches and cigarette ends in it. My other granda smoked both a pipe and cigarettes but did not have a spit jar! His wife would not have allowed him to. Granda loved his garden; we knew not to play near his roses at the front of the house and to be careful playing on the grass at the back. Lyndsay used to climb up the clothes poles and granny would let us play at tents, pegging her sheets into the ground. Often ruining her sheets, but she never minded. Granda had plants galore in the house and also in the greenhouse that he had built on to the side of his shed. My granny would often find her lost wedding china plates underneath his geraniums or her brand new expensive Tupperware containers being used as mixing bowls for his paint. He would paint the clothes poles, the handles of his tools and the bird table all the same colour whenever the notion took him. One of their neighbours had a West Highland terrier that barked all the time, my granda would only take so much of it; then he would go out and launch his heavy sweeping brush at the neighbours fence, giving the dog a fright and shutting it up for a while.

We spent lots of time with our paternal grandparents when we were younger, in fact my grandparents looked after me when I was around six weeks old for a week when dad took mum, Lyndsay and Andrew abroad to Tenerife to give my mum a rest after her caesarean section. Maybe that is why I was always so close to them. There are photos in the family album of Lyndsay and Andrew playing in the black volcanic sand on a Tenerife beach. I did always managed to get my granda to tell me that I was his favourite, he was mine. Most Saturdays we would watch the wrestling together, when Giant Haystack and Big Daddy came in to the ring, the crowd, my granda and I would chant easy, easy! I thought that it was real wrestling but it was play-acting for the crowd and the cameras.

I will never forget my granny on my dad's side telling me the heartbreaking story of the babies that she had miscarried before she had my dad and uncle. She was in tears and it had me crying too, she told me that each time she lost a baby was just awful but the last one she had carried for a little bit longer and when this pregnancy ended she told her husband that she wanted to see her daddy, who lived just next door.

There had been a family rift because my granny had left the family home to get married to my granda, her father was not happy about this as it would mean that there was no woman in the family home to look after the men. He eventually took on a housekeeper who in the end became his wife after she fell pregnant with his baby. When his own daughter had needed him to hold her he would not come around to see her, even after she had lost yet another one of his grandchildren. My granny had lost her own mother to diabetes at the age of eleven and she had to give up her schooling to take on the mothering role within the home. She had to work very hard at taking care of her older brothers and her dad, cooking, cleaning, washing and mending their clothes that they wore when they worked down the coal pits. That story still always brings tears to my eyes. I cannot get over the fact that her dad would not come to see her when she really needed him, especially after everything she had done for him. Granny gave me her mum's wedding ring that she also wore; I have never taken it off since she gave it to me.

Some of the things my granda did were crazy but always made us laugh; maybe we should not have laughed, as some of the things were dangerous. He would get the toothpaste and the deep heat muscle rub muddle up, not noticing until he went to put his false teeth back in to his mouth. I had a sore ear one night when I was staying overnight and my granny asked him to heat up olive oil on the cooker, he touched the electric ring to see if it was getting hotter because it did not go red straight away. Yes, it was heating up and he burnt his fingers. The olive oil was to be heated; a piece of cotton wool was to be dipped in it then put in to my ear to encourage the infection out of it. I also took my fireworks to their house one Guy Fawkes night, granny and I stood on the back door step while he placed them in to the grass lawn and lit them with his matches, when they did not automatically shoot up in to the air he went back to see if they had maybe gone out and needed to be re lit, he nearly got his face blown off. He had no patience, neither has my dad! My granny would have a clear out and put bags of my granda's shoes and clothes in to the rubbish bin, the next thing you would see would be him taking them all back out of the bin. Especially his shoes as he did not believe in banking his money, he would keep it in the wardrobe stuffed in old shoes. That is one way to lose your money.

My granda was average height, with big broad shoulders, the whitest hair I had ever seen; I thought he was very handsome, in fact I thought he was the best thing since slide bread. He taught me how to look after plants, although I am still not great at that; but I keep on trying. Granda used to fry packets of bacon for us on a Sunday morning after we had stayed over; we used tons of tomato sauce, granny used to stay out of the way until the 'murder scene' had been cleaned up. My granny on that side had the softest hands and I was convinced that they could heal any ailment, she was so small and cuddly, she had curly salt and pepper hair, and just how you would imagine a granny to look like! The little white stool that my dad had used in his bakers van was originally my granny's, she had to use it when she was going out in one of my dad's high cars, like his Land Cruiser or his Vauxhall Frontera. Every month she would measure me up against the wall beside her chair; she would mark how much I had grown on to the wallpaper. Lyndsay and I had a great time one day at their house playing with granny's red lipstick and a white face cloth, we drew all over our faces, looking like coco the clown and we then used the cloth to wipe it all off before starting again. I think the cloth had to go in the bin along with what was left of our granny's lipstick, she never every wore make up, we found that lipstick in one of her old tins. My grandparents celebrated their golden wedding anniversary, fifty years married is some achievement, they had their picture taken for the local newspaper, they must have felt like celebrities; they were a good-looking couple. I knew that I was close enough to ask my granny anything; I asked her opinion about when she thought I needed to get my first bra, she helped me organise myself when I had an unexpected period while I was staying over and we had many personal conversations over the years.

My mum was quiet shy about talking to us about sex etc as her own mum had not talked to her about these things other than to tell her not to get pregnant before she got married. She bought me a book to explain things to me when I first started my periods. The strange thing is that when my own kids got old enough to have conversations about those subjects mum was very open with them, much to their embarrassment.

I was gutted when at the age of ten when my granda passed away, he had suffered a couple of strokes before he died but the last one put him in the hospital. I thought that he was a superhero, indestructible. This was my first experience the death of a close family member. The night before his funeral I went with my dad, his uncle and my granny to see my granda in the church; where we paid our last respects. My dad still has the key that locked his dad's coffin. I remember his funeral so well, it was a really cold day and at the graveside I took my granny's hand just to let her know that I was there beside her. Afterwards she asked me if I could see any of the small white coffins that they had buried previously; their lost little babies. I am so glad that I did not, for her sake and for mine.

I spent more time with my maternal grandparents as I got older; I went on many shopping trips on a Saturday with my granny and auntie to Edinburgh, resulting in me being addicted to shiny things in a jeweller's window now. I would love to work in a jeweller's, imagine trying all the rings, pendants and bracelets on before the shop opened or after closing time. I do not think I would have much left in my wage packet, as I would want to buy all the lovely shiny things.

My maternal granny also worked as a dinner lady at the high school that we all went to, she would slip me sweets under my plate of chips, it was nice to see her everyday, her hair was white with a yellow tinge at the front as she was a heavy smoker; slim and average height the same as my mum although I think that my mum took her looks from her dad's side of the family as my granda was tall and slim with dark hair. My auntie was small with dark hair and both daughters had the same features as their dad. My granda still had my mum's piano and would let me 'play' it all day until I managed; eventually to play 'The Entertainer' and 'Happy Birthday' maybe the reason he put up with it was because he was deaf in one ear; a result of being knocked off of his bicycle years before. I know now that I was extremely lucky to have both sets of grandparent while I was growing up, many people do not have this privilege. We enjoyed many holidays together as a family, not a complete family as my paternal granda had passed on, Lyndsay and Andrew did not want to come and my auntie Pauline probably enjoyed the peace of having the house to herself.

The rest of the family went to Oban, in Scotland for a week, my mum's parent and I shared an apartment and my own parents shared another one with my dad's mum. We went to visit Iona, a small island just off of Scotland, on the local ferry boat, when we got nearer the island the ferry had to stop and down anchor as the water was too shallow to get any closer to the island, the passengers then had to be transferred on to a smaller boat that could take the tourists straight to the island. We watched some of the passengers being transferred from the ferry's deck above, before we decided if we were going to go for the trip. My dad was concerned about his mum's mobility issues; she could not walk far and used a stick due to her arthritis. Anyway we decided that the trip was worth it, we had come this far; so we all got transferred onto the smaller boat, I say transferred but it felt more like 'grab and throw'. My poor granny did not have time to think about it before she found herself on the boat. We took our trip around Iona on a horse and carriage; it was well worth it. Iona is so peaceful and the scenery was beautiful. Then we had the 'grab and throw' to get back on to the ferry to travel back to Oban. That night my granda had a few too many whiskeys and he ended up falling in to the bath, he was unhurt and all he kept saying was 'Im sorry mummy' to my granny. I think she was going to choke him but we helped him out of the bath and put him to bed. I bet he was very sorry the next morning!

Many a happy Christmas was spent as a family and we had parties at New Year, usually ending in the conga around the house more often than not started off by my dad or maternal granda. I enjoyed listening to their stories about when they were young and learning things from them, my granny on my mum's side taught me how to knit, how to put button holes in to my knitting and I remember swimming for the first time in my pants at the seaside on a day out with my granny, granda and my auntie. Granda was paddling beside me with his trouser legs rolled up as he encouraged me to kick my leg and swim. Granda used to go swimming with us a lot once we could all swim, pretending that he was Jaws, the killer shark from the film, chasing us in the pool. On a Sunday my granny would make a huge dinner, homemade soup, roast beef, roast tatties and pudding, we were all so stuffed afterwards that we had to have a sleep. I was the only one who ate the desert; I did not want to share the jelly or rice pudding. After my granny became ill my granda took over the Sunday dinners, he must have been watching her because his meals were just as tasty. My auntie always did the dishes but Lyndsay and I took turns at drying them. After dinner was eaten and the kitchen was clean my auntie would wash and dry my hair for me, sometimes colouring it too. By my first year at High School I had been many shades of blonde. I think that she took the stress of her working week out on my scalp; I kid her now that my scalp has just recovered.

My granny and granda on my mum's side lived just across the road from my dad's parents so it was handy for the grandkids to go between their houses either on foot, by bikes or roller skates. There were plenty of laughs in that house too; my granda knew how to annoy my granny, he would read aloud the credits at the end of the television programmes, would sing his made up songs or would sneak a whiskey and when he was caught by granny he would let her smell it, she would make a face at the smell of the neat whiskey and he would say 'see, I told you it was not nice and you think im enjoying myself'. I remember us all playing card games; my granny thought my brother was so talented at the game memory until she noticed he would stretch and roll underneath the glass topped table to look at the cards before he took his turn. My auntie, who was still living at their home had a friend across the street that would knock the door asking if she wanted to join her when she walked her dog, Tickles. When my granny would hear the door she would tell my auntie Pauline to keep her at the door and not to let the dog in the house, as it was old and really smelly. Pauline and her friend Elaine used to take Lyndsay and Andrew to the swing park, they would teach them to swear and encourage them to be cheeky.

Here are just two of granda's songs that he would sing to make us kids laugh and to annoy my granny.

Bluebells are bluebells	There was a wee man
Bluebells are blue	Who peed in the pan
Bluebells are bluebells	The pan was too wee
Just because they are blue	He peed in the sea
(Each verse the same)	The sea was too wide
	He peed in the Clyde, and
	All the wee fishes swam up his
	backside

5

moving house for the first time

We moved into a larger four bedroom house in the village as my parents thought that it would be better for us to be within waking distance to the school, nearer to the bus routes and to all our friends. I was still at primary school and Lyndsay and Andrew got the bus to high school with their friends.

In my early years at primary school I was selected to be an angel one year for the Christmas nativity play and the following year myself and another girl had been asked to sing a lullaby to baby Jesus. I was not nervous when I was an angel because there were a few of us but when it was just another girl and me singing, in front of the school and all the parents who had come along to watch, I felt sick. My mum said that my face became whiter and whiter as it got nearer the time where we had to go up on to the stage. It was my first experience of singing in public.

One particular girl in my class made my life hell during my primary school years; one day she would be your friend, the next she did not speak to you and she would stop everyone else speaking to you. There was a small group of us girls who played together at school and we would each get a turn at being ignored until one week we got wise and ignored her. She did not like it one bit and went crying to her older sister who begged me to speak to her and to get the rest of the girls to do the same and like a softie I did just that. A few weeks after me being a softie I could not believe it when she got one of her 'friends' to threaten me, telling me that when the bell rang to say school was over she would be waiting outside to hit me, I told my teacher about this and she just brushed it off; telling me not to be silly. After sitting for the rest of the day worried about when the bell rang she was not even outside waiting on me. I had worried for all day for nothing. It was nothing like the anti bullying policies that schools have now. Things continued like this throughout my primary school years until I decided that I just did not need the hassle and I never spoke to that girl again after that, she was nothing but a bully and who needs that in their life?

My mum's mum had taken me to get my ears pierced when I was much younger and I had let them close up. Now I wanted them done again and decided that I would do it myself. I got a bit carried away with the piercing earrings that I had kept from the previous time and ended up with three holes in each ear. It was not that difficult to do, all you have to do is push the piercing stud through the two layers of fat on your ear lobe. A bit painful during but I thought it was worth it.

This new house meant that Lyndsay and I had our own bedrooms, mine was a small room but I was overjoyed at the built in bed with the curtains around it. I felt like a real princess. There was also a smaller television room where we could have our friends around, giving mum and dad the lounge to watch their own programmes or to chat. Eventually when I out grew my bed, mum and dad moved downstairs in to the extra television room, their bedroom became mine and dad had my small room made into an office. Mum never minded when I had friends staying over, often there were four girls sleeping in my room, giggling all night. Their mums were not so keen to have us all sleep over at the same time.

My dad had settled well into his new role as a double glazing salesman, often winning cars and holidays when he was awarded salesman of the month, you could say he was very successful; not bad for someone who was so shy that my mum had to ask him out for their first date.

One Halloween dad rented some horror films and we had sweets and popcorn, dad had bought me a ghost mask and Andrew had a rubber mask that looked like an old lady. When mum went to the kitchen to get juice for us, Andrew had sneaked upstairs into my bedroom, which was directly above the kitchen, he was dangling the rubber mask out of the window on a piece of string and mum screamed so loudly we all ran through to see what was wrong. Andrew had not finished his nonsense that night, after we had watched the films and finished our treats we got ready for bed, I went in to my room first and as I turned off the light Andrew slid my wardrobe door open; he had my ghost mask on, I nearly wet the bed.

One year the family holiday took us to Tenerife, Andrew stayed at his friend's house, as he would rather do without a tan than be seen by strangers with his family, as it was not cool! We stayed in a huge hotel, rooms next door to each other on the tenth floor, Lyndsay who was a daredevil used to hang across the balcony and nose into mum and dad's room. Thinking about it now it would have been really easy to slip and fall the ten stories, the things she did were frightening. The scary thing was that mum and dad went back to see the hotel years later when they were on another holiday and it was not there as it had been demolished due to structural damage.

Lyndsay being skinny bet me that she could fit in to the suitcase and I could not because I was chubby, so I said ok, you go first. When she was inside the case I zipped it up and started to roll it about the bed before I pushed it on to the floor, she was not happy and had a few bruises. That was what she got for saying I was chubby. After we had our dinner one night I got my portrait done in chalks, dad said it was worth the money to have a few hours peace. Charming! We did the tourist trails while we were there, going up the volcanic mountain, well Lyndsay and dad made it all the way to the summit, mum stayed with me after the traumatic cable car ride. I did not want to go back down in the cable car but I had no other choice, it was awful. While shopping in the market my mum was offered a leather handbag for her pretty bambino, the man was touching my 'real' blond hair while he asked and mum just smiled, pulling me towards her and walking away. I bet she wondered if the handbag was made of good quality at times!

Mum went shopping every Wednesday to Edinburgh, she would buy me girly outfits and I would rush home from school desperate to try them on. I would waltz down the stairs holding the new skirts or dresses out, letting them flare out, pretending I was a princess. When I got older I used to go to the hairdressers with mum and I loved it. I would watch the girl who did my mum's hair and wishing I were her, making my mind up that I would become a hairdresser when I grew up. I did have the gift of the gab after all! Mum would let me blow dry her hair for practice, she would use the curling tongs on mine and when she was not looking I would be dying Babies hair with her mascara then giving Barbie a hair cut with the kitchen scissors and sometimes she ended up with her hair melted around mum's tongs. Extremely Bad Hair

Day Barbie! I am not sure that every little girl would want one of these.

I would say that I was musically confused when we stayed in that house, I had heavy metal, i.e. AC/DC, Meatloaf and Black Sabbath, coming from my brother's room, Otis Redding, Prince and also The Smiths coming from my sister's room, mum played classical music and 60's so I listened and liked it all along with whatever was in the music charts at the time. This is probably the reason that I now have a varied musical taste, which is not a bad thing. Car journeys when I was younger gave me the opportunity to learn all the words to my parent's tapes – Del Shannon, The Everly Brothers, Neil Sedaka and any other 60's music that they had. I loved to sing and was not as shy to do so in front of my family, my granny asked me to sing Eidelweiss for her friend once, I was so nervous as this was my first time in front of a 'stranger', when I was nearly finished the song the woman burst into tears. I stopped singing, thinking that she was upset because my voice was awful, I did not realise until my granny told me later that her friend was upset as that song reminded her of when her husband who had passed away had taken her to see The Sound of Music. That same friend of my granny's used to make cakes and tablet, one day she came across to the house and asked my granny if I would nip around to the shops for her as she needed more ingredients. I said I would not go; my granny was not pleased and rightly so. What I did not explain was that I was worried about going, what if I could not get what she needed, did not get the right thing, ran out of money, went to the wrong shop or I got lost? I just was not confident to go by myself, it was not as if I was really young, I was such a worrier then. I still feel very bad today about not doing this small task that would have helped my granny's friend.

My dad and mum took Lyndsay and I horse riding on the Saturday's when the caravan season had ended. It is an expensive hobby as you hire the horse, the hats and pay for the time that you go out on a trek. I was a bit scared, sitting on top of large animal that you have hardly any control over; so the instructor lead my horse as we went on a trek. That was fine until a brightly coloured cart came around the corner of the road; the horse that I was riding got spooked and started to buck, I fell off and that put me off the horse riding experience. Mum was never as keen as my dad was anyway, so we stayed at home. It did not put Lyndsay or my dad off; they went back the following week. Lyndsay took her boyfriend at the time along too; off they went on the trek that the horses were used to, following the lead horse with the instructor on. At the end of the trek only my dad and the instructor arrived back at the stables on time as Lyndsay and her boyfriend's horses had bolted. After more than an hour of worrying the horses brought them back to the stables, as they knew the route home. They were head to foot covered in mud but they had huge smiles on their faces and I am sure that the horses enjoyed taking another route home. They had even been jumping over fences and galloping through fields. Madness, but Lyndsay and her boyfriend had a fantastic day!

My dad cousin still lives in Yorkshire; their house is about an hours drive away from the theme park Alton Towers. We went many times to spend a weekend with the family and to visit the park. Dad's cousin is a brilliant cook, her chocolate cake is divine. One visit to Alton Towers that sticks in my head is the time that we were on the log flume ride, near the end where you get your picture taken coming down the last slide and end up soaked at the end. Dad was sitting in the first seat of the ride and when the girl in the kiosk at the top of the slide handed him the ticket that he would need to collect his photo at the end of the ride, he stood up inside the ride because he could not hear what she had said. She could not tell him to sit down quickly enough; she must have thought we were Scottish tourist idiots. When we went to collect our photo the girl in the kiosk at the bottom could not speak for laughing and the other girl had mascara running down her face. It is a pity that the photo was not taken when dad was standing up inside the ride at the top of the slide, which would have made a better photo than the one of us soaked at the end. He has never lived this down and I bet the girls who were working in the kiosks that day still talk about the Scottish man standing up asking the girl to repeat what she had said when all she did was hand him a ticket. Our Yorkshire relatives would visit often and we did too, all the kids got on and we used to get each other to say 'purple worms' in the different accents, laughing at how different it sounded. We still visit back and forward, now it is myself and my younger cousin that have the kids, it is just really good that the family keep in touch.

I remember one of my birthdays just before I finished primary school. I woke up to find a square box wrapped in pink paper with little roses on it. I took particular care of opening this parcel, as I wanted to keep the wrapping paper to cover my schoolbooks; I was overjoyed when I discovered the latest Walkman tape recorder, it turned the tape for you so you did not need to open it and do it yourself. It was a cool present.

During my first year of high school I had made friends with a girl called Sarah, she had went to a different primary school from me. I went for a weekend in Blackpool with her dad and step mum; we enjoyed our meals out, the amusements and our time staying in the guesthouse. I made many new friends when I started the high school, meeting people from other areas and getting to know them.

I had my first boyfriend at the age of fourteen; we met through friends, a group of girls who hung around with a group of boys. It was at this age that my virginity was 'taken' from me, I say taken not lost, as it was not my choice. It happened one evening when our friends were downstairs watching the television in his house; his parents were out and we were sitting in his bedroom listening to music. Yes, we were kissing and cuddling, which we had done previously but I had no idea that it would turn in to sex, it was what 'he' wanted and although I was sore and started crying, I thought that it was the 'norm' between boyfriend and girlfriends! We kept on seeing each other for a couple of years afterwards then we broke up when he went off with another girl. If I knew then what I know now I would have told someone, it was not two innocent kids fooling around, it was statutory rape as I was underage and he was seventeen. How I wished I had waited until I had met someone I really cared for and who felt the same way about me until I gave up what was mine to give away. It should not have been taken from me that evening. After it was over I fell down the last few stairs inside his house as my legs were like jelly. He did make sure that he did not run the risk of getting me pregnant though; at least I did not need to worry about that afterwards. Thinking about that now makes me believe that he had planned the event.

6

moving to the massive house

The family moved into their third home when I was fifteen years old. A custom made mansion by many means, my fathers dream, a house designed and built exactly to his requirements, and what requirements they were! You could say we lived a very good life. We did not have ponies but im sure if we had asked it would have been different. As I am now allergic to horses, a pony would not have been a good idea anyway. I found that one out after going out for a walk with my granny and granda after we had eaten out large Sunday dinner. I stroked a horse that we had walked passed and then I must have rubbed my face, the next thing I knew was that my lips and my eyes were all swollen up, I felt that it was difficult to breath also. Our walk ended there and when my granny and granda got me back to their house, granny made me eat ice cubes and placed a cold face cloth on my face. A magic old-fashioned cure. I never went near a horse again.

Our house was built behind the original mansion house, which had been made into flats, there were other house built within the estate i.e. barn and stable conversions. The majority of the people who lived in the flats and houses were stuck up; in fact one man who lived in the renovated coach house was a pain in the backside. His complaint was that when we drove passed his house his window was being splashed by the dirty water in the puddles. There was only one road in and out of the estate; so everyone passed his house. Lyndsay and I were in the house on our own one-day and he came to the door to complain, he was pretty scary. Lyndsay held our dog, Rover by the collar when he was ranting on about his dirty window; he did not know that our fierce looking Alsatian was blind in his remaining eye. After that visit we thought that he deserved something to complain about so Lyndsay, Dad and I waited until it was dark, took a box of eggs, splattered his window and then we lifted the road gate off of the hinges and place it across his front door. Wish we could have seen his face when he opened his curtains the next morning to the egg covered window and also when he tried to leave for work, opened his front door to discover the gate. Funnily enough we did not have a bit of bother from him after that.

For a birthday treat my mum and dad took me for a weekend in London; we went to see The Phantom of the Opera, I loved it and I have seen it twice more since then. I was also treated to a Neil Sedaka concert in Glasgow for the same birthday.

When the film Dirty Dancing first came out we would have the soundtrack blaring at the weekends when our parents were away at the cabin. When the stuck up flat owners called and asked us to turn the music down Lyndsay would say ok, no problem and then turn it up louder. The other residents of the estate must have though that we were common and that we should be living in council houses, nowhere near them. My brother would get grumpy with us playing the Dirty Dancing soundtrack and the film over and over, dancing around to it, he used to say 'if you put that rubbish back on I am going away to my bed', we kept playing it over and over and he never did go away to his bed. Those weekends were fun, a small group of us would have a drink, my tipple was dry Martini and lucozade or wine. Beer or vodka was the tipple for the boys, we would watch films, have take away meals and because we lived outside the village, Andrew, Lyndsay or I would take turns driving when we went to the local pub on Friday and Saturday nights. We would fill the jukebox with money and get drunk in the local public house, singing loudly and laughing. I was underage when we first started to have these fun weekends and when I celebrated my eighteenth birthday the bar staff bought me my first legal drink. I always did have my big brother and my big sister to look after me; although I sometimes had to look after them. Andrew still talks about the night that we were thrown out of the pub early when a group of our friends who were sitting on the other side of the pub started to throw the beer mats at us, we retaliated, just having a drunken laugh, it is nothing like what kids get up to now when they are out. Now I sound really old! Many a good night was spent when we were all out together, I can still laugh at some of the things we got up to.

When the family ordered a meal to be delivered to our house from the local Chinese takeaway restaurant it would be hours before it got to us as we lived outside the usual delivery runs, having no street lights in the estate did not help matters either and trying to explain where to send the driver was a nightmare. Once we were waiting for hours, we had called twice asking where our meal was and we were told that the driver was lost but it would not be long. When it eventually turned up we were all starving, mum and I started to put the meals out onto plates and while we were doing this Andrew lifted his bag of chips out of the plastic bag that the meals had been delivered in, so he could put them on to his plate. The bottom fell out of the paper bag, which was containing his chips. Being quiet but quick-tempered and probably because he had waited so long he threw the bag and the remaining chips in to the open fire and stormed off to bed. We all just went quiet and looked at each other then burst out laughing, he still gets reminded of this now.

When I was in my last year at high school I woke up one morning to a very sore right eye, it was bloodshot red and painful when I looked at a light. My dad took me to the local doctors and they sent me to the Hospital where they did lots of test on me, including blood test to see if I had arthritis. The hospital admitted me overnight after they discovered I had Iritis or Uveitit, which meant that my iris was inflamed. They gave me two different types of drops every two hours after they had injected a steroid drug straight in to my eyeball. They froze my eye with drops before the injection but it was really hard to try and keep my eye still when I could see the needle coming straight for it. I suffered from this condition three more times within the space of a year, twice in my right and once in my left eye and had the same treatment. The arthritis blood test came back as negative though.

While I was still using my eye drops I went on holiday to Oban again with my mum and dad. I was been sitting at the open window of the apartment watching the ferries dock, and a seagull landed on the outside window ledge, it leaned inside and stole the small plastic bag with my eye drops in, my dad said we would know which seagull it was as it would be flying around with one of its wings covering its eye. We still laugh about how greedy the seagull were. Big shock for that bird when he discovered that what was in the bag he had stolen was not edible.

I had an incredibly scary experience at high school one day at break time, a group of us were hanging around in the corridor waiting for out next class to start; laughing and chatting, I was eating some polo mints. The next thing I recall was that I started to cough, my friends thought that I was joking with them; when

I tried to get their attention, I could not stop coughing, the polo mint had stuck in my throat. I was so scared but luckily enough for me polo mints have a hole in the middle or I would have been unable to breathe. My friend took me to the school nurse and she made me eat a piece of bread after a hot drink did not dislodge the sweet. I had a sore throat for the rest of the day but otherwise it was as if nothing had happened but I have not forgotten that day or eaten polo's since, I was petrified.

During my high school years I had an extremely good male friend, we were so close. I would say that we were best friends, we talked about everything and even wrote long letters to each other. We spoiled it though by crossing the line from friends to boyfriend and girlfriend and of course when it did not work out we could not go back to how we had been with each other before. I was sad that this had happened and I sometimes wish I could go back and repair it as we were really good friends. You live and learn, so they say!

When I was 16 my granny, my mum's mum, became really ill with lung cancer, even although she had trouble catching her breath she still managed to tell me off if I had too much make up on thought. I was working in a salon in Edinburgh and training to become a hairdresser so I had to have my face and hair done. On the train to work I never wore my make up and I managed to get a half return ticket for a few years after I should have been paying for an adult's ticket. My granny passed away in her own bed at home, with her husband and daughters beside her; we all went to see her at the funeral home, to pay our respects. She looked really made up, all I could think about was that she would have hated having so much make up on.

Dad worked so hard as a double-glazing salesman, we often only saw him at the weekends or really late at nights, but our mum was always there for us as she stayed at home to look after the house and family; you could say we had the traditional family upbringing. I had weekly singing classes at a theatre school, we each received brand new cars when we passed our driving tests, all-first time around, we had foreign holidays, weekends away to our caravan where we used our speedboats and later the caravan was changed to a chalet/cabin. My siblings and myself kept our lifestyle quiet at school; we denied our dad and mum having new cars, the speedboat being parked outside the house. Dad would go and order a new car without telling my mum and just appear with it. Usually she got a massive bouquet of flowers a few days before this happened. We definitely did not brag, we were not like that. We could have ended up as bully magnets if we did.

By the time I had passed my driving test my brother had bought himself a Suzuki Swift and he had offered, one day to take our paternal granny to visit one of her friends not far away from her house. His car just died on him half way through the journey, he did not have a mobile phone then so he had to leave my granny in the car and he had to walk to get help. Other motorists were stopping to see if they could help, it must have looked strange that an old lady was sitting stranded inside a sporty car, she told us afterwards that she only opened the window a tiny bit to talk to the people. It turned out that there was nothing wrong with his car, it had an engine cut out switch down by his feet and he had hit it by accident. He did not even know that his car had this switch installed when he had bought it. A wee exciting day trip out for my granny!

Myself and two of my friends decided to book a holiday to Corfu for a week. We went self-catering and shared a two-bedroom apartment. We did what teenagers do on holiday, ate out, got drunk, slept most of the day and got burnt in a panic to get a holiday tan. Of course there were boys who chatted us up but we stuck together and enjoyed our break. I must have talked too much to one of these boys, as he appeared when I was waiting to get my train home from my work one night. He followed me home and the outcome of this was that my dad gave him some money to get lost, which he took but turned up at my work the following day. I told him to go away or words to that effect! Stalker alert!

After training for nearly three years for my dream job as a hairdresser and having being trusted to do a basic cut, colour or perm within the salon I ended up suffering from contact dermatitis and had to give up my dream. It was strange that the allergy had taken so long to come on, the last style I did was a perm and I remember nearly crying as the lotion ran up my arms as it reacted against my skin. I was devastated at having to give up my job; I had never ever wanted to be anything else. The skin on my knuckles and fingers had nearly all come off, my skin was raw, and I looked like a burns victim. I had to get someone to put cream all over my hands and arms, put on cotton gloves and then clear sort of breathable plastic gloves on top of that. I cried as this was done due to the pain I was in, it was awful and took many months to get better. Getting myself washed and dressed was a nightmare. I missed doing the job of my dreams, being the guinea pig for any new colours that came out; I had my hair green, red and purple at one point.

I even went black when I was a bit Goth at one point. The fun that we all had while we were run off of our feet on a Saturday! We would have a few bottles of wine in the staff room and once we had cleaned up the salon after the last customer had gone, we would quickly cash up the till and then we went to the pub. I used to get the last train home on Saturday nights after having a few 'lemonades'. I did not even worry about walking home on my own from the train station, in the pitch dark, through fields. There were no streetlights to guide me on my way, as our house was some way out of the village. I would not do that now, but when you are young you have no fear. Once I had passed my driving test, my dad bought me a brand new bright red Vauxhall Nova, I would drive it in to Edinburgh and park on the outskirts of town then I would get the bus in to the city centre. It was much better than taking the train.

I was lucky that I had my English and Secretarial O Grade passes to fall back on, surprising really since I did not try very hard at the school, I just had my heart set on hairdressing. So I felt that I had to apply to and attend a local small college, I gained qualifications in information technology, personal computing, business applications and business administration. I was also put on a placement via the college and the company employed me when my placement finished. I sometimes came home at lunchtime from my new office job to have something to eat with my mum, when I arrived at the house one lunch time I noticed that I had a flat tyre, mum and I had never changed a tyre before so we called my brother who worked five minutes away, when he arrived we must have looked a right pair, my mum with her yellow rubber gloves on and me trying to get the wheel nuts off with the caps still on them. Women! My brother changed the tyre, shaking his head, not saying a thing and went back to his work. Dirty job's that involve cars are boy's jobs anyway!

With my mum being at home all day she was there for her dad to stop by for a small whiskey when he was fit enough to walk up to visit and also for my dad's mum, who could lift the phone if she ever needed anything. My granda still continued to make the Sunday dinners and would even make soup through the week and take some over the road to my other granny. They would have a cup of tea and a chat everyday together, they had both lost their spouses and it was company for them.

One day my mum got a call from my granny, she was in a panic as she was desperate for her eleven o'clock cup of tea but the doctor had just been out and had given her new pills, my mum asked her why she did not just have her tea as usual and my granny explained that the medication information leaflet said that she was not to work machinery while she was taking them. She thought that this meant that she must stay away from the kettle. My mum went out to see her and reassured her that she could use the kettle, washing machine and the cooker whilst taken her new medication and that the warning was for people who work with large machinery or drivers.

On a Sunday during the church service I would help out with the crèche, there was mainly toddlers and babies to look after, the older children played with the toys or games; amusing themselves. Once the service was over the older children attended the Sunday school within the church.

7

the proposal and the in laws

Every young girl dreams of her wedding day, the dresses, flowers, fancy hotels, diamond rings, then the house and babies come straight after. I was no different, in fact I knew even before I was ten where I wanted my wedding reception to be held and my dad had listened. Every time we passed the Scottish Hydro Hotel I would say 'that is where I want my wedding'. The groom appeared in my life just before I had my eighteenth birthday, my friend's brother's friend! We met in the local pub and he bought me a drink, how romantic.

I have now been separated from him for seven years and divorced for five years but I still cannot say his name so lets just call him 'arse' because that is as good a name as any and very apt.

My marriage proposal happened in the same local pub where we had met, just inside the doorway, not in front of anyone. How could I refuse when he produced the engagement ring that I had collected from the shop that morning, out of his jeans pocket? So you could say that it was not a surprise! I was three months off of turning eighteen and I had known him only three weeks at this point, well I say 'known' but that is a huge exaggeration, really I did not have a clue what I was getting myself into. The things that girls do for diamonds! My dad thought that I was joking when I announced my engagement, on my own I hasted to add; and I cannot say I blame him. A bit of rough from the council estate where nobody works but they have lots of kids, satellite television and brand new cars. At least I had two years to "really" get to know him before the wedding day arrived. The engagement ring went in to the bin a few times and you would have thought that I would have seen the blindingly obvious light after lying to the police for him about a window that he had smashed in temper, this window was in his mum and dad's house. Sadly no, I saw no light. Even when my brother in law to be made a pass at me I still wanted to go through with it; one moment I was dancing with him, the next he had his tongue down my throat and I was the one who was marched home and given a telling off for behaving like a whore. It was years later that I was given an apology from my loving husband when he discovered his brother had been sleeping with his own wife's best friend and also their next-door neighbour's wife.

I really did have my blinkers on during this time, I was the one who wanted to get on well with his family and I tried my best by baby-sitting their cheeky monster kids and by being their taxi service with not so much as a thanks for it. I have a severe phobia of the reptiles that start with the letter S and when one of arse's nephew's and his underage girlfriend had a baby daughter; the baby basket was being kept beside the tank, I could not get out of the house quick enough. My mum was invited out to his parent's house for a cup of tea; I have never seen her look so uncomfortable. My mum thought that his dad was rude and ignorant as he kept turning the television up while 'the women' were talking and that the house needed a good clean, she sat on the edge of her seat all the time we were there. I tried to make a good impression by buying my mother in law to be an expensive box of mint chocolates for her Christmas one year only to be told that she 'did not like f*c*ing mints' as soon as she opened the parcel, I was gob smacked, I did not buy her f*c*ing mints again but I noticed that she did enjoyed pan drops, that are MINT. Speechless!!

I still enjoyed my singing within the Theatre School and I had also joined an amateur dramatics company. I loved my twice-weekly singing sessions but I did not want to perform during their amateur dramatics shows, so I only went for the practising. This was until I was told to give it up and to spend more time with my soon to be husband. Stupidly I did as he asked!

My fiancé and I went to buy our wedding rings in Edinburgh; I noticed that one of the smaller shops just off of the main shopping street had a sale on so we went to have a look in the window. I spotted a ring that I liked, I also liked the half price tag, it also had the matching man's one on sale but he was not happy as it meant that if we bought both of our rings on that day from that shop he would be unable to get the doc martin boots that he had seen in the shop a few doors down. I was allowed to get my ring and he got his boots. Priorities! This meant that I had to rush about looking for a wedding ring for him, it was not an easy task as he had big gorilla mitts (probably useful when he was dragging then along the ground like a Neanderthal) he refused to come with me ring shopping again as he had already been once.

8

the wedding

The day of the wedding finally arrived, the cars were at the door, the dresses were on, hair was pinned up and the photographer was taking random pictures. My mum was helping me, Shannon and Lorna who were my two bridesmaids and my flower girl, Emily get ready in my old bedroom, I was feeling sick with nerves and it probably did not help that myself and my bridesmaids had been up most of the night before, chatting and laughing. Making sure that all us girls were ready my mum then had to rush to get herself dressed as the photographer was asking for her. When she was ready and standing in the living room, she was telling my dad that it was "ridiculous that the photographer was here so early" just as the man himself tapped her on the shoulder! I think that she was stressed out, with all the rushing about and helping everyone, but her nerves would not have been calmed by the fact that she had just stabbed herself in the head with her hatpin, resulting in an attractive bloodstain on the inside of her pale green hat. Nobody could see it and she did not tell me until after the wedding meal. It was like a carry on film.

The time came for dad and I to get into the Rolls Royce wedding car, we were both on the verge of tears and the chauffer then asked me what I would do if arse was not at the church. Very funny! The thought that entered my head was not of devastation at being jilted but of how much money my dad would have lost. That should have told me everything I needed to know and if my dad had said I did not need to go through with it then I would not have. So romantic! More like so unsure and naïve! Unbeknown to me, the groom and his best man were smoking cannabis around the back of the church, this being the reason that the chauffer had asked me that question; as he had not seen the groom at the church entrance greeting our guests. My dad was taking me to the same church where he married my mum and they had their three children christened. It must have been an emotional day for him; he was giving away his youngest child. It was the local village gala day and a silly rumour had been going around that I was arriving by helicopter, the crowds were out and when we tried to turn in to the church entrance all I could hear and see were people banging on the car. I felt like a child murderer getting taken to court. When I got out of the car my veil blew off of my head and my dad caught it, another omen!

The wedding was a princess's dream, no hitches apart from the hatpin accident and then the grooms inability to perform his marital duties after dark due to his alcohol and drug intake. How I wished now that I had went to my parents hotel room when my wedding reception was over, they had gate crashed another wedding reception after mine and then they had room service and a party in their room with our Yorkshire relatives. I was left to undo my hair and to struggle out of my dress, alone. My mum tried to leave her bloody wedding hat in the hotel dining suite where we had our wedding meal but a waitress came running after her the next morning with it, she did not have the heart to tell the young girl that she had meant to leave it behind. Never mind,

I had two weeks in the sun to look forward to; little did I know that it would only be a week as my period dared to come early and spoilt the 'honeymoon', so home early for me! My parents eventually agreed to come and pick us up a week early from the airport; they thought that I was only joking when I called them to ask.

My sister and her boyfriend eloped and got married at Gretna Green on the border of Scotland and England; four months after my wedding. They had been planning their wedding for a while but had not told anyone, they sent a letter to my mum and dad and also to his mum and family; telling them that they were away getting married and then going to the Caribbean for two weeks on honeymoon. My parents were hurt and upset. My granda, my mum's dad thought that my auntie Pauline had know all about the wedding and had went along as it was the one and only time that she had attended her works night out. When the newlyweds arrived back to my mum and dad's home they could not understand what the big deal was! It was what they had wanted, a quiet private wedding. My mum and dad threw them at party to celebrate afterwards.

Not once did the any of my soon to be husbands family help when we got a council house, an upstairs two bedroom, four in a block flat, which was run down and filthy to say the least. My dad, mum and I worked really hard to clean it up, we even wall papered the inside of the cupboards. Arse painted half a ceiling and had to stop because he was shattered! My parents paid for every single thing that was put into making the flat a home and it was lovely when it was finished. Although it was a dirty job and the house was freezing until it was lit; I enjoyed having an open coal fire.

It was a pity that the house was where it was, probably the second roughest street in the village. It turned out that our neighbours who had the downstairs house; wanted the house that we had been given for their daughter who had just had a baby. This family also had a semi detached three bedroom house across the road from us, where they ran a pub from their garage; customers paid for their drinks by giving the 'landlord' their giro benefit checks. Our lovely neighbours dug up the path, leaving a huge hole at the gate, they lifted the paving slabs, breaking most of them and they blocked in our car; but the worst incident happened one night when my dad came to take photo's of the hole that they had dug at the gate, this was to be the evidence that would be shown to the council. The whole family ran over the road after seeing my dad with his camera, the mother of the clan punched my dad in the face and gave him a black eye and the father threw a slab at my soon to be husband and chased him down the back of the garden. I was upstairs trying to call the police when all this was happening. I could not believe it; my dad was blocking the front door, stopping the mother and daughter getting into the house to get at me. I was calling the local police stations number and not 999, as I did not think that it would be classed as an emergency. The police knew the family very well and they told me never to hesitate in calling 999 whenever something happened, as assault was an emergency. I had never had to deal with the police before so I was a bit naïve about which number to call. This was the only time my dad had been in a fight in his life, standing there with his collar, tie and blazer on. My father was protecting me while my big strong man was running away. Of course by the time the police arrived it was all over, they took statements and then left telling us that we would have to give evidence in court.

The court case was an eye opener but the family were charge, however they did go on to glue our front door locks when we were on our honeymoon, but we had no evidence of that. My brother kindly stayed in the house when we were away because we were scared of what that family would do. The council eventually offered us a swap nearly six months after the event, which we took as by that time I was pregnant and I did not want to have a baby in that house with those neighbours, I imagined that I would have my baby outside sleeping in his/her pram and that they would steal the pram or the baby. I still stay and now own the house that was offered as a swap.

I have always disliked smoking; I made it a rule that I would not have anybody smoking inside of any house that was mine. Arse and his entire family smoked, I told him that he could smoke outside, as I did not want to breath in his fumes or have my house smelling of smoke. His family did not visit very often as they could not go without a cigarette for any length of time, which did not bother me at all. As it turned out our baby son had asthma and this was yet another reason why I did not allow smoking within the family home. When we visited his family they smoked whether you liked it or not, even in front of babies and young children; the females even smoked while they were pregnant.

You would come out smelling of smoke and I hated it, I hated the fact that my kids were clean and tidy until they had been out to visit their family.

9

babies

Unfortunately trying to get pregnant did not come naturally for me and after various doctors tests I was told I needed some help, my ovaries were not producing eggs at the correct time; or as my mother in law would put it 'it must be your fault, there is nothing wrong with any of my boys' and 'you can only get pregnant if you both come at the exact same time'. How I kept a straight face I will never know, I wish now that I had asked her what she meant about coming together, if only! I did ask her about what happens when women get raped, becoming pregnant and I was told that they must have enjoyed it. Speechless!!

My mum's dad was very ill with bowel cancer while I was pregnant but he still managed to keep his daft sense of humour; I cut his hair in his kitchen one day and had left him to change his top, the family were in the living room and you should have seen their faces when he came through saying 'look what she did to me', his head was covered in tomato sauce and it look like I had tried to scalp him.

Eventually I managed to produce an heir almost a year after my wedding, a son. Three days after I had the baby I turned twenty-one, which was ok because my caring husband and his brother celebrated for me as I was kept in the hospital for nearly a week. My parents were thrilled, my mother in law less so as it was 'just another boy'! I was happy it was over and that the baby and myself were ok, it was traumatic thirty hour long labour before I eventually met my son. Many procedure had to be carried out before they realised that the baby was too big for me to deliver naturally, some of the procedures still make my eyes water now. Arse and my mum were there during my labour but arse was unable to attend the birth of his child by emergency caesarean section as he had a sore back sitting in a hard chair overnight. I had no choice and my front was killing me. My mum had to get dressed in green hospital scrubs and paper shoes; I would not let them start before she was there holding my hand. She had a good look at what they were doing, probably because she had a caesarean section with me and it would be interesting to watch. It is the weirdest feeling in the world, someone tugging and rummaging inside your stomach them pulling a tiny human out of your body. When they held my new baby son over the sheet that was draped over my chest; my first thought was that he had red hair, but he had not been wiped clean of the blood yet. My epidural was wearing off as they were stitching me up and they had to stop while they topped me up with more drugs. My mum was the first person to hold my baby and afterwards when she went to find 'daddy' he could not be found inside the hospital, he was celebrating outside with his friend, cannabis! Now that is what you call concerned, his wife and son had only been rushed to theatre, as his baby's heartbeat was getting weaker!

Unfortunately just three weeks after I had my baby son my granda, my mums last parent passed away. Very much missed and still loved, my mum probably had mixed emotions at this time as she was ecstatic at becoming a granny but very sad at losing her dad after a long battle with cancer. My sister's friend Sam looked after my baby while I went to the funeral, which was good of her as she had a ten-month-old baby of her own to look after. Arse and I collect him after the church service and we went back to my mums where I changed and fed him. Arse was complaining that I was taking too long and that this would mean that all the food would be finished by the time we got to the small reception. I wanted to scream 'Bloody sausage rolls and sandwiches are the last thing on my mind'. I had lost my granda, I was not very well, had a baby to care for and this idiot I had married was harassing me.

My mother in law had a vast knowledge of child rearing as she had five boys and was always on hand for advice. Unfortunately, her last child had been a stillborn baby boy, when she spoke of this tragic experience she shrugged her shoulders and said 'it was just another boy'. They did not even hold a service for this little baby. Her advice was given whether you wanted it or not. For example; you must squeeze the baby's cheeks together when they yawn to prevent lockjaw! The only person I wanted at that time was my own mum, the postnatal depression kicked in big time straight after the birth but I was not willing to admit it to anyone, all I could think about when I looked at my baby was 'where did the baby come from, I have had my appendix taken out so it is not my baby'. When I was discharged from the hospital I stayed with my baby at my mum and dad's house for a while, they were great. Even when I went home to my own house they were always there for me, they would have the baby on alternate nights to give me a rest. It took me a long time to admit that I had postnatal depression and to seek the doctor's help. My loving husband was not a great help; in fact he was not in the house much in the evenings or the weekends. The doctor doped me up on anti depressants for about two years and I remember in the early days

I did everything that I had to for the baby but I was convinced that he cried because he did not like me. I called my mum very late one night for her and dad to come and just take the baby because I knew that he would wake up and cry. I am not sure what would have happened if my parents had not have been as supportive as they were then, I could never thank them enough.

When our baby son was six months old, arse left us and went back to his mums, as he could not handle the pressures of being a new dad and having a postnatal depressed wife. Arse visited his son everyday and then twice a week after I had to go and seek advise from a lawyer when he told me he would take the baby from me and not bring him back, then after about a year he moved back in. I would not say that things had improved much between us; he still went out ever evening and to the pub on a Saturday night. I had applied for a job with British Telecom at their directory enquiry centre and my mum looked after my son when I started working during the week. This was another reason for me taking arse back, I wanted him to take the pressure off of my mum, I knew she loved looking after my baby but I felt that if arse could collect him from my mum's house, even an hour before I finished work then it would be easier for her. If she had known this I am sure she would have had a few words with me!

At Christmas that year my mum as usual had made the family meal, we were all sitting chatting at the dinner table, but my son, who was a toddler by then was getting restless so I let him leave the table to play. He like to take all his clothes off, a stage that they all go through, and he stood naked having a conversation with Timone and Pumba from the movie The Lion King which he watched constantly. I was telling the rest of the family at the dinner table that I was worried that he had imaginary Timone and Pumba friends as he talked to them all the time. Everybody started laughing at me as I was talking about how I hoped that he would grow out of it; he was so animated with the conversation that he was having, talking to them as if they were sitting on the sofa. I had no idea that my mum and dad had bought him a Timeone and a Pumba soft toy and that they had sat them on the sofa, my toddler was talking to his new toys. I could not see the sofa from where I was sitting at the dinner table. My face must have been a picture and the rest of the family were laughing so hard they nearly wet themselves.

On the 13th of March 1996 I was working at the British Telecom directory enquiries call centre when we were handed around a memo about a gunman shooting children in Dunblane Primary School, we were advised on what to say if a member of the public called to ask for any numbers concerning this incident. By the time my shift ended seven primary one children had been killed and the police marksmen were on the scene, I remember a male colleague saying 'I hope they get the bastard', a twenty minute drive home to my mum's was all that it took for 'that bastard' to shoot and kill the entire class of sixteen children and their teacher; who was found laying across them, trying to protect them. I took my two year old back to my house, put him down for a nap and cried as I watched the breaking news. Thomas Hamilton took the cowards way out and ended his own life using the same gun that he had used within the school. I have never hugged my toddler as much as I did on that day. How could some evil person go into a primary school and do that, it is only forty minutes by car from where I live, unbelievable! From that day on all Scottish schools operated a locked/swipe door system so that this would never happen again. We can only hope.

The first dirty caller I received at the BT call centre was in my early days and in fact I asked the man to repeat it, as I had not fully heard what he had asked for, what a doughnut! I soon learnt how to react to the weird callers, usually it was the evenings; we would say that as soon as it hit 10pm it was the three P's; pizza's, pub's and perverts. A directory enquiry was free from a call box at that time. Usually if one of us took a dirty call then the same sick individual would call for the rest of the night, jumping around the call centre from telephonist to telephonist until he was either bored or relieved. I did enjoy my job with BT and I was with them for over four years until I became pregnant with my daughter; this pregnancy also required assistance from the doctor. I had to take a double dose of the fertility drugs before I got pregnant for the second time. One of the routine blood tests came back as abnormal, the midwife visited me at my house and explained that it was nothing to do with the fertility drugs, it may mean that I was carrying twins, a down's syndrome baby or a baby with spina bifida. I had to wait a full week before I could have a more detailed scan. My mum was with me when I was told the news and she went with me when I had the detailed scan, it was amazing, we could see the baby's fingernails and the cupid's bow of his/her lips. Arse did not want to go! We did ask about the sex of the baby, I wanted to know after all the worrying, but the sonographer said she could not tell with the way that the baby was positioned and if I really wanted to know I could go and eat something sweet and come back. I just wanted to go home, I was so relieved that my baby was perfectly healthy. The very next day I woke up with a baby bump, it was as if I did not want to think about being pregnant and after the relief of the clear scan the bump just appeared. Normal clothes one day and maternity clothes the next! I suffered with extreme heartburn during this pregnancy and my mother in law told me that it was a sign that the baby was hairy! I nearly bit her head of and said 'it will be a bloody monkey at this rate'. Stupid woman! The same happened as with my son, my brand new baby daughter spent her first few days at my mum and dad's house, my son was there anyway as my dad had been looking after him. Daddy/arse went back to our family home on both occasions though; I think he was on his own; I did not care. His loss! Anyway that first night I woke to breast feed my daughter and realised that Dolly Parton had climbed in to the bed, I could not get the baby near me to give her a feed, I had been bleeding and my hormones had kicked in too so I did what any young mum does and woke my mum. The first thing that she did was go downstairs and wash (with washing up liquid and tap water) a small bottle that we had bought for the baby to drink water from and she filled it with cows milk that she had heated up in the microwave. That kept the baby quiet and content, mum told me not to tell the midwife! Stripping the bed and then tucking her daughter and baby granddaughter into bed, my mum went back to her own bed, job done. My daughter had no unpleasant after effects from that night, in fact she was hardly ever ill and my son whom I wiped clean all the time, making sure he was spotless was always catching every little bug or cold that was going around.

As a family we did have times where life was semi happy, we took our son to Corfu for a week when he was just a one year old, what sticks in my head about that holiday was when nobody else would get into the swimming pool as it was cold water but when our baby showed them all up by jumping into the water with his inflatable boat around his body; holding his dad's hand, well guess what? The next thing you know the pool was packed full of holidaymakers. Children under the age of two travel abroad for free but they do not get their own seats on the plane, they sit on a parents knee; I had my son on my knee. On our return flight I had a top on which fastened with studs, my baby son took great delight in pulling mummy's top open. I am not sure what worried me the most, being arrested for flashing when we landed or being arrested for drug smuggling for the cannabis I had hidden inside my bra that arse told me I had to take for him. We managed another trip before our sons second birthday. This time we had two weeks in Majorca; nothing really sticks in my head as eventful from that trip, apart from the fact that it was far too hot for a toddler and being away from my mum and dad for two weeks was just way too long. I was so glad to see them when we got home and they had missed their grandson so much.

One night after I had bathed my daughter, changing her nappy, putting her in to her baby grow so that she was ready for her bed, I carried the baby bath through to the kitchen to empty out the water. My son had been helping me wash his sisters hair and I left him to talk to her when she was laying on her changing mat on the floor. I came back in to the lounge and my son had unfastened her baby grow, had her legs in his hands and a new nappy under her bottom. I wish I had taken a photo as it looked so sweet. When I asked him why he was changing her again he told me 'she had wet herself' and I asked him how he knew, he looked at me as if I was silly and said 'Mummy, she told me she had'. Priceless times!

I got the two kids Christened on the same day, when my son was three years old and my daughter was four months old, she wore the robe that mum had bought for Andrew, and then Lyndsay and then I wore it at our own Christenings. My son had his smart white shirt, black trousers and Thomas the Tank Engine bow tie and braces. We had a party after the ceremony. The divide between the families at the party was very clear that day, as they did not mix at all. Sitting together at separate tables.

I would love to have got my son Christened as a baby, wearing the robe but I would not have remembered it. When my daughter started to roll over, hold her head up, crawl and then walk, I kept asking my mum if my son had done all of these things at the same age as I could not remember it happening. It is like my mind totally blanked out all of the early months, that still hurts me but there was nothing I could do then and nothing I can do about it now. What hurt me the most was when my son fell or hurt himself he would run straight passed me and go to my mum to be made better.

When my daughter was six months old I lost my last grandparent. My granny, my dad's mum had been in a nursing home for a few years and she had gradually gone down hill. She ended up in a wheelchair and needed lots of care, which she hated. It was another sad loss for the family; I am so glad that she had got to meet both of my children.

10

becoming the real me again

It was the last family holiday abroad to Ibiza for two weeks that really got to me; we went as a family of four. It was hard work trying to keep two young kids entertained in the baby pool while daddy was at the bar and when the kids were asleep during the evenings I was in the hotel room with my book. At least the kids can say that they did have holidays abroad with their parents, for the first two I had to use my childhood savings to pay for the holidays and arse got a bank loan for the last one. I still sometimes wonder what he did with his wages; I know that I never saw anymore than the £100 a week that he expected me to stretch.

Constantly being told I was useless, thick and having to ask if I could make a cup of tea or go to bed in my own house, having my shopping receipts checked to see what time I was at the shop; was getting a bit much by this point, plus the kids saw and heard this happening, I wanted to stop the learnt behaviour. Having to wear my engagement, eternity and two wedding rings. Just so that I did not forget I was married, as if I could! To me this was proof that his cannabis intake was causing paranoia and that I was in a damaging relationship, we all were. It was not healthy!

He actually told me that a husband could not be charged with raping his wife; it was a husband's right! This was usually after he told me he felt 'the need' but had not had a shower that day but would offer to give himself a rub around with a baby wipe or run his private parts under the tap! If I was having my period at the time I had to give him light hand relief. How could I say no, oh that is right, I could not because I was his wife and he had rights! I was also told that having sex with the woman on top hurts a man, that my arse was too fat to have sex from behind and that people who say that they have sex more than once at a time are liars. If you have done it correctly the first time you cannot do it again and again because you cannot get another erection, which means that the people who brag about having sex all night long have not done it correctly the first time. I have since found out that this is all pure rubbish!

As long I had his coffee fit for him to drink, the kids homework done and the dinner at least cooking when hubbie got in the door after his work it was all ok. Usually I did the kids homework on a separate piece of paper and all that they had to do was copy it into their workbooks, it saved time and any upset. However, I would get upset if the kids had homework with those reptiles starting with the letter S was in their books, I had to call a teacher once because my son had a reading book with one of them on the front cover, I could not even pick the book up so I called the school to ask if he could have another book after I explained my reasons for not being able to help him with his reading. I know that I did far too much for the kids, I would lay their clothes out, cater for them like a waitress and I even cut their toe nails until they each left my house. They did not have any chores to do and they usually got what they asked me for, many times I would do without so that they could have things. My mum would tell me off for being as soft with them.

I felt like a single parent, especially in the evenings; the minute the kids went to bed hubbie was out the back door and to honest with you I did not really care where he was going by that stage, it saved me from getting shouted at or even having to look at him. I would spend my time with him walking on eggshells, as I never knew when he would kick off, it all depended on his cannabis intake. He would tell me that he was going to visit his friend or that he had to go back to his work to unload the cars off of the transporter. I knew that him and his friend were smoking funny cigarettes during his visit, that is if he was with that certain friend. In an argument he once accused me of using him to have kids; he definitely was from good breeding stock! Pedigree chum more like!

I got my first tattoo at this point, I remember arse not being pleased as I had a teddy and the kids names tattooed on my lower back, he questioned why I did not get his name included, I told him that the kids would always be my kids but that he was not for keeps. I must have been having a brave day that day, or maybe I was still recovering from the pain and not thinking straight.

My family knew that things were a nightmare at home but they did not want to interfere as arse took it out on me, not physically but mentally, there were times when I wished he would just hit me and get it over with. There was one occasion where he slapped me hard across my face; it was when I was holding our son as a small baby. I cannot remember what I had said or done. He would behave very differently when we were in other people's houses but as soon as we got behind our own door it was very different. Outsiders would often tell me how lucky I was that he was such a caring husband and a very involved father. It stuck in my teeth but I just smiled. What was the point in telling people the truth; nobody knows what goes on behind closed doors. My mum said he had more faces than Big Ben. The arguments were pretty bad; the kids must have heard us fighting when they were in bed at nights and I am not ashamed to admit that he did scare me, still does if I am honest. It took me many years to be able to have eye contact with people and to be comfortable with it, even now the smell of chewing gum reminds me of him as he was always chewing it, probably to get rid of the smell of cannabis from his breath. He used to tower over me or the kids and point at us when he was telling us off, he used to tell us to shut up often, I knew that these were the two things that I would put a stop to as soon as we separated. My sister had an idea of me making his dinner one night with dog meat and telling him it was a curry, if only I had been brave enough. I would have been scared that he would have know by my face that something was going on, great idea though.

By this point I was not very well, I had been having severe gynaecological problems since the birth of my daughter, my own doctor had tried lots of different medications and after exhausting various treatments she ended up referring me to a surgeon who told me that I needed to have a partial hysterectomy at the age of twenty six. I suppose I was lucky that I had a son and a daughter, I never planned on having any more kids anyway but having the decision taken out of my hands was devastating at such a young age. My mum and dad looked after my kids when I was in hospital, which could not have been easy, my son had just started the school and my daughter was toilet training, mum also brought them to visit me every afternoon, I missed them so much, it did not matter how much pain I was in I made myself walk with them to the hospital ward doors so I could cuddle them goodbye. Having the operation was the best thing that happened although I was not saying that when I was recovering. I did feel so much better straight away but then my friend brought her new baby boy to visit me at home, and it hit me that I would never hold my own baby again. I overdid it doing housework, lifting my daughter and ended up giving myself a double hernia. I was given a telling told off by the nurse at the local medical centre, what are you supposed to do when you have a lazy arsed husband and two kids to look after though. My job with British Telecom had ended, as they would not keep my job open for me; the weekend shifts that I worked were in high demand. I did worry about what I was going to do now for employment and money. Then I saw an advert in the local newspaper showing that a plumbing service in my village had a vacancy for a part time receptionist, I called them, had an interview and got the job. I worked from 4pm until 8pm Monday through Friday; I liked it well enough, especially when the daytime office staff went home at 5pm. I could then put the television on, have a cup of tea or do some exercises after I had done all of my duties. The manager was an obnoxious piece of work, his manner with the staff was shocking and in fact he had me in tears one night when I called him about a problem with one of the plumbing jobs. The owner had told me that the manager was on call during the evenings and that I was not to hesitate in calling him if any problems arose. The following day he denied speaking to me in any such manner when the owner had us both in the office, little did he know that I had already spoken to the owner as soon as I got home after my shift the night I was upset by him. My auntie had just started her training day on the Saturday after this had happened and when she heard how he had treated me she left and I did the same the following week as I had as much as I could take, it was bad enough being treated like that at home and I did not need it in my workplace.

I never went on nights out with friends, in fact I gave up all of my friends when I got involved with arse as it saved him moaning. I did however get out of the house when the kids were a little bit older thanks to my mum and also when both of the kids started school. I got addicted to the gym and attended around ten-fifteen hours a week. I regained some of my confidence and looked pretty darn good, even if I say so myself! I was so addicted that even after I had a benign breast lump removed I only took two days off the gym instead of the recommended full week. I just needed the high and I had met some really nice people there. It was my outlet.

From the minute my two kids started the nursery and the primary school I always volunteered to assist as a parent helper on their nursery or school trips out. I did miss them not being in the house during the day, I would look forward to them coming home from the school and I always had a cuddle, snack and a drink ready for them when they did get home. I enjoyed spending the time with them and their friends; we went to the theatre, the zoo and the seaside. My daughter would get jealous if one of her friends took a shine to me and she held my hand to make sure a certain friend did not get the chance to, as I was her mummy. I attended all of their parent's appointments with their teachers, enjoyed going to their plays; mum and I really enjoyed watching them both in the nativity plays. These plays were different from when I attended that school as the Mary and Joseph story was far too traditional at this point and did not meet with the needs of all the children or their parents. Different religions or cultures had to be considered. When my daughter was in her first year at the nursery she was an angel in the nativity play and my son; who was in primary one was a reindeer, he wore a furry suit. They looked so cute and did very well at their parts, my mum took her video camera to record the play so that the rest of the family could see it too as each child was permitted just two tickets each. The angel and reindeer year was a problem for my mum to video as my son was at one side of the stage and my daughter was at the other. The kids were only happy when the camera was on them; my son went off stage at the end with a grumpy face and would not give us a wave.

My big brother came to my rescue regarding a job, he had worked for the same engineering company since he left High School and offered me a clerical job two days a week, job sharing with the girl in the office who also had a little daughter the same age as mine. The factory itself had eight machine operators; the office had four administrative employees including myself, plus a lady, a pensioner who came in two mornings a week to clean. She was lovely and told everyone what she thought no matter what! It can be very handy having your brother as the boss! I was even 'allowed' to Christmas nights out, as my brother would be there to make sure I was 'behaving' myself. I do remember one year, wearing a little black dress, I felt great but I obviously had to try it on for approval from my husband before the event, he suggested that I wear a jumper over it as it was too low cut and he said I would give people the wrong idea by wearing it without a jumper. I did not look one out! I am certain that he put me down so that I would end up not going out after all. I did not give him the satisfaction and I had a great night out.

At long last I had a full time job and I could prove to myself that I was capable, not thick or stupid, I was clever and useful. Yes, I enjoyed my role as a mum but I needed to find the strength to find myself again. I was also given the opportunity to dress smartly instead of being in jeans but this had its drawbacks as I would get told off by arse for dressing up for the old bas**rds at work and not for him. I really enjoyed that job, the staff all got on well, the nights out were enjoyable and I really clicked with two of the engineers in particular, Adam, his main role was stock, despatch control and calibration, I used to try and teach him the latest dancing moves I had learnt at the gym's dance classes. We had a few laughs at his two left feet. The other man, worked on the machines. John and I had a really good friendship; we would spend our lunch breaks putting the world to rights. I would confide in him about my life at home and he always made me feel better, he said that I deserved much better, should not pay attention to what arse said as he knew I that I could do anything I put my mind to, he saw in me what I could not see myself, not then anyway. Adam was simply a good friend at work, although we did swapped emails and became friends on Facebook later on; I often get email cards from him. John and I had something different. At that time we were both married so there were boundaries that we would not cross but the attraction was there. We both felt it. A couple of times he gave me money just to treat myself to something, im not talking about a lot of money, just enough to buy myself a bottle of nail polish or a box of chocolates. Although he did pay for 'that' little black dress for the Christmas work's night out. It was lovely to be treated like a worthwhile human being, that sounds a bit deep but with my home situation being the way it was I was just enjoying being spoken to nicely, being called an intelligent lady and feeling like laughing again. John is a gentleman, one of the nicest men I have met, one you can trust to talk to your face and not look down your top! Like a couple of the other engineers in the factory used to do, boys will be boys! I kept that to myself as arse would have went ballistic if he had know I had male friends or that other men had been looking down my top.

My mum agreed to look after my two kids after school while I went out to work again, I loved getting back into the office environment and I stayed there for just over five years. I could not have worked or looked after my kids without my dad and mums help, not only did they look after them while I went out to work, they babysat if I had a night out (very rare) and also bought them clothes and shoes because they knew that I was given just £100 each week from my husband, the father of my children from his wages to pay for food, clothes, rent, bills, essentials etc. My dad said it was like the story of Jesus with the fish and loaves. Arse kept the rest of his wages to himself and I could not tell you to this day what he earned and never saw a pay slip in all the years that we were together. He had his secrets; I was probably better off not knowing what he was spending the rest of his wages on. If the kids were away for the weekend with my mum and dad I would be left sitting myself at home while arse had his usual Saturday night out, you would think that we would have went out together as we were child free but no.

It was a normal Thursday at work, the 11th of September 2001, when the salesman walked into the main office to announce that an aeroplane had flown straight through one of the Twin Towers, New York City's World Trade Centres; he was saying that it must be a joke. Then we were stunned when the radio announced that another plane had crashed into the second tower, and that a third plane had crashed into the Pentagon, a fourth had crashed into the ground near Pennsylvania after passengers had taken the hijackers by surprise and brought down the plane. It was unbelievable, of course we only heard the news on the radio, the towers both collapsed and later when we all got home and watched the footage on the television's news it was like something from a disaster movie. People were throwing themselves out of the windows from the burning towers; others stood watching in shock from the pavements until the towers began to slowly crumble to the ground. This, even today is an unbelievable sight, watching people die and being so helpless. I cannot watch the television when they show it again without crying, imagine what these people must have been thinking, knowing that they were going to die. A terrorist group called Al-Qaeda and their leader Osama bin Laden admitted it was their doing. Nearly 3000 innocent people died on that day.

In 2003 I turned thirty and decided that since I had 'celebrated' my twenty first birthday in the hospital having my son I was going to have my twenty first and my thirtieth as a combined party. This was going to be my year where things were going to change for the better. I had a great night with my family and friends, danced the night away and had a good few drinks, I walked back home to the house with arse and the kids around one in the morning, my feet were so sore from dancing I had to take my heels off and walk home barefoot. It sure did help the gutted feeling of turning thirty! My life began at thirty though!

11

gaining confidence

By that point my sex life was non-existent as a result of a smear test when the nurse looked up and asked if I knew that I had a Sexually Transmitted Disease. I was for once lost for words and mortified as the nurse at the local doctors surgery was the mother of one of my old school friends, which made it even more embarrassing, plus she was a friend of my mums. I also had to explain to my mum why I needed her to look after the kids on the day I had the appointment at the STD clinic. My mum was so angry and wanted to say something to arse but I asked her not too, for my sake she did not have words with him about it. Humiliating, and it got better as arse said I must have caught it at the gym, this was said while I had my legs up in stirrups as the doctor in the STD clinic was examining me. Considering that I did not even use the toilets or showers at the gym, it must have been one of his mother's topics of expertise. Along with 'men cannot have sex again after a vasectomy', 'men can be raped by a woman as fear can give them an erection'. 'Nipping can give a person cancer'. Seriously, the woman could have done stand up at the Apollo. The tickets would have been a sell out. Anyway, after many months of embarrassing extremely painful treatment I knew I was clear, arse refused to give his permission to be checked by any doctor. I found that strange.

I got back in touch with an old school friend though Facebook. We started off meeting for lunch and now we are as her mother says 'as thick as thieves', meeting often, texting many times a day, sharing secrets and stories that we would not share with anyone else. Marianne had moved away to Glasgow after she got married and had come back home after separating from her sh*t of a husband, in fact she lives just along the road from me; I had passed her door everyday and I did not even know. Marianne became a close member of my family and was very good to my kids; she did not have the honour of meeting arse.

On Boxing Day 2004 a massive Tsunami hit Phuket, Thailand, 4812 confirmed dead, 8457 injured and 4499 missing. What a shock to anyone who had any compassion. The instructors at the gym decided to hold a fund raising day, a full day of classes – Body Pump, Body Step, Body Jam, Body Attack, Body Combat, Body Balance. I am unsure as to how much was raised but I know that it was a great success; arse; my brother and the kids went swimming while I attended the six hours of fitness classes. I enjoyed that day, yes it was tough going and I was unsure if I would be able to move the next day but it was for a worthy cause and as usual it gave me my fitness buzz, the adrenalin rush that working out always gave me. I was fine the next day, still buzzing in fact and not sore at all.

12

getting my life back

I finally took my brave pills one Saturday night and arse left but only after I had agreed that we would have a break, not have a complete separation. It was sneaky on my part but oh so necessary. He actually told me that if he found out that I had been seeing someone else or met someone else within six months of him leaving then he would tamper with the breaks in my car and to remember that his hand fits around my throat. I had to do something, we had been arguing for years, it was not good for the kids to see or hear and it was not healthy to be in that sort of relationship. I knew that when he left that night that he would not be back to live in the family home. That was not a pleasant evening; the kids were seven and eleven, their dad called them downstairs from where they had been playing in their bedrooms, telling them that 'their mum' had something to tell them! I explained to them, while arse sat I in tears, making me out to be the bad one, that although mum and dad could not get on together anymore, we still loved them very much, it was not their fault, and that dad was moving out for a while but they would see him often. Our daughter kept on playing on the lounge floor and our son sat beside his dad crying then told me that he hated me and stormed back up to his bedroom. It took arse nearly twenty minutes to get out of the gate, he stood, in tears waving to his son who was watching from his bedroom window, I wanted to open he door and tell him that he was making things worse, hanging around. I thought that things were bad living with him; I had no idea just how hard it would be to get rid of him.

I think of that night often, I was so proud of myself. After I had got the kids off to their beds I stood in the kitchen, flicking the kettle off and on, asking the cat if we should have tea or go to bed. In the end we had a cup of tea in bed and it was great to decide all by myself and not having to seek permission! It sounds so silly now but the relief was immense. Yes, it was very upsetting for the kids as the family had broken up but I knew that things would be better eventually. In the beginning the only thing that changed was that he did not eat or sleep in the family home, which was not good for anybody so I went to a lawyer with my dad for advice and she sent him a letter with set times and days for him to see the kids. I was so scared about him receiving this letter that my lawyer sent me a copy on the same day so that I knew when I received mine he would have his. My auntie Pauline came with me once to the lawyer, as a statement was required to back me up about the mental cruelty. She gave one hell of a statement. Being just like my mum she did not hold back, she told the lawyer exactly how I had been treated over the years that I had been with arse, unlucky for some thirteen years! This started a war, he wanted to change silly things just to get to me, he just did not realise that it was his own kids that were suffering, he took me to the family court stating that he wanted full custody of our son but not his daughter. The kids ended up with their own lawyer who asked them who they wanted to live with, they both said that they wanted to live together with their mum; the lawyer and judge agreed that I should have full custody as it would be in the kids best interest. I had a seven year-old little girl crying and asking me why her daddy did not want her and an eleven-year-old son who began to self-harm, cutting himself and not eating. It was heartbreaking. I could not tell my daughter that the reasons why her dad did not want her to live with him was because he wanted to hurt me or that it may be because females were second-class citizens as far as her dad's family were concerned. Ignorant inbred behaviour from arse, his brothers and nephews treated the women that they were with in the same way, even his own dad treated his mum with no respect, he would click his fingers and tell her to get in to the kitchen and make him a coffee and she did as she was told. He would greet the dog with more emotion than he did his own wife when he came home from his work.

To top off my embarrassing STD episode I found empty condom wrappers in arse's underwear drawer when I was packing up his clothes, he must have been playing at finger puppets with them. Why would he need them anyway, his wife had a hysterectomy and we were not even having sex. Thank goodness for my sense of humour, if I did not have that I would have ended up in a locked psychiatric ward.

By this time I had taken my wedding, engagement and eternity rings off and I swapped them for a pierced belly button and another tattoo around it. It was great to be able to do anything I wanted now. I did not need to ask permission to do anything; it was all up to me. I think I took my new freedom to the extreme when I got my nipples pierced though. I took the nipple piercings out after around six months; I just did it because I could. I accompanied one of my friends when she got her 'downstairs' bit pierced; my legs were shaking for her. When the man who did it gave the table a spray and wipe once it was over, and then asked me if I was next

I said definitely no. Only the doctor and your man friend should see that part of you!

My daughter had joined a cheerleading squad and was really enjoying it; she did really well when she participated in their Christmas show. I loved her purple velvet outfit; her pom-poms and her dancing shoes were expensive as were the classes but I did not care as she enjoyed her hobby. That was until her dad asked her if she felt fat compared to the other girls within the group. I could not believe that he would say that to her, I fact the next thing I knew it had knocked her confidence that much that she did not want to attend the classes after that, giving it up after over a year.

My son had many hobbies, ranging from fishing, football, army cadets, and athletics. He did not attend any of theses for very long. Both of the kids enjoyed swimming lessons and they both gained a certificate for their rookie lifeguard lessons, the also did well at karate lesson until their dad decided that sitting watching them train was not the quality time that he should be having with them so he stopped them going and spent quality time with them while they watched the television at his mums and he smoked in the kitchen!

After a weekends visit with their dad, the kids came back really upset. My son burst into tears as soon as he saw me and as I held him he told me that that his dad had punched him in the face because he did not listen to him, I wanted to take this further but my son was scared of what would happen, as it would make his dad angry. My son told me that when he got bigger he was going to punch his dad in the face to get him back for punching him, I told him not to lower himself to his dad's level. My daughter had been bitten by the neighbour's dog on the leg and was told not to tell her mum. I called the local off call doctor to see if any treatment was required but as the skin was not broken it was not necessary for her to be seen or for a tetanus booster injection. Every time they left my house to spend time with their dad I was worried sick, they should have been safe with him but it was never ending stress for me. No wonder I was finding grey hairs! There was another occasion where the kids were in the car when their dad was buying his drugs; I knew that this story was true because I have been the one waiting in the car while he nipped in to the drug dealer's house. I had a dreadful day when my daughter kept texting me counting down the time until she came home, as her dad was grumpy, she had to do this from the bathroom as he did not like them contacting me when they were with him. Sometimes if he was in a bad mood he would take their mobiles off of them. My daughter's birthday fell on a weekend that she would be spending with her dad and she was so excited, when she came home I asked her what they did and what her present was (as the kids were not allowed to bring anything their dad had bought them for birthdays or Christmas back for me to see); she told me that she did not even get a card and that her dad said he had no money so they sat in the house. I was so angry; I asked if he was sucking on a cigarette as he was telling her he had no money!

The first time we went before the judge I was terrified, arse was sitting straight across a desk from me, in a suit I bloody paid for. I had not seen him for over a year and I just had visions of him grabbing me if he got his temper up. The second time in front of the judge; it was ruled that the children should remain in my custody and the judge also stated that Christmas day would be spent with me and that the kids would see their dad on Boxing Day. Arse stormed out of the court room, my mum had went along with me that day and when I came out of the court room she asked me what happened as arse was so angry, all red faced with temper. My mum was beaming, glad that at last he did not get what he wanted. He said he would fight the judges ruling and fight for his son, then after all the court hearings, lawyers letters, other lawyers being involved and the kids being upset he changed his mind and decided he did not want custody of his son after all. I could not believe it. It was a coincidence that this was around the time when he had met his next victim, I mean female friend. There were a couple of times when he did not even turn up for the court hearings, a waste of time and his own money that he blamed his own son for making him spend! It was the hardest time of my life and I could not do it again but all I can say now is thank god for DIVORCE. The divorce officially came through around a month before he married his new wife; I have to admit it would have given me great pleasure if it had not come through in time.

I bought a double blow up bed and a sleeping bag each for the kids so that they could have their friends to stay over now. It was too embarrassing to have their friends stay before their dad had left because I did not want their friends to hear us arguing. Resulting on the kids getting talked about at school or outside. They had many friends to stay over, I must have been like my mum, allowing them to stay up most of the night, eating sweets and watching films or playing video games.

My sister had been taking care of the kids one day while I was working and it had been arranged that arse would collect them from her house, she has three small dogs and I could not believe it when she told me that just before they were due to be collected she had given my daughter a 'dog poo' bag filled with chocolate spread and told her to pretend that it was real and that she had forgotten to put in the bin. Lyndsay said that she told her that it would be really funny if she then opened up the bag, dipped her finger in to the chocolate spread and ate it. I nearly wet myself when she told me about this and then again when the kids came home and told me their dad went off of his head. His mother was nearly sick and also did not find it amusing.

Many months after the divorce was finalised and as I was putting the dinners out, I stopped and said to myself 'you do not get left handed cutlery'. I had just realised how gullible I had been. That arse had been adamant that he needed certain cutlery when he ate; he made a massive fuss if it was different cutlery. He could not help me iron as the iron was made for a right-handed person and so was the vacuum cleaner. I felt so stupid for saying nothing and just letting these things go at the time but it did save me from getting shouted at. Also, I was numb to all of his nonsense by then.

To celebrate my divorce I had three small stars tattooed on my right forearm, they represent my son, my daughter and myself. I wanted it done mainly because we were all stars to have come through such an awful time. Tattoos are very addictive. I also had a triquetra symbol tattooed on to my right ankle at the same time as it represents 'all three put together as one'. I thought it was fitting at the time.

13

bettering myself

I decided that I wanted to better myself, I applied to college to do an introduction to nursing course and I got in. I was over the moon. I was still working with my brother and it was sad to say goodbye to all the staff but I was moving on to something bigger and better. John was beaming as he always told me that I would get into college and I could do the course work with no problems at all, his confidence boost gave me the motivation to try and I will always thank him for that. After six months on the introduction course and doing another year on the access course I had the qualification to get into university. It is the best I have felt in years, my confidence was through the roof and I also changed my name back to my maiden name. Things were on the up and my life had turned around completely. Huge stepping stones for me.

The very first assessment that I had to do during my introduction to nursing course was a nerve wracking experience, I hardly slept the night before I handed it in, but I did and when the tutor told me that I 'wrote very well' my confidence soared. There was no going back after that, I knew then that I was not 'thick'; 'useless' or 'stupid' and I knew that I could do anything that I put my mind to. John was right after all, I kept in touch with him by text message and he visited occasionally. He said that he could see the person I had now become in me all those years before when we had first met, he was so pleased for me that my life had turned around.

I felt that I had to add this very first essay just to show that this was when my life turned around and I started to say 'I can' instead of 'I cannot'.

In this essay I will be discussing stereotyping, prejudice and discrimination, about how when all these are linked together and even on their own can affect people's lives. I will then go on to describe how this affected my school life only because I was lucky enough to come from a wealthy background.

Stereotyping can happen when people are put into groups and classed as the same type or when we assume people belong to the same group and this can give us a certain image of that group of people.

Prejudice occurs when we have negative and/or irrational feelings towards individuals or groups of people. We often do not want to admit to others that we have these feelings and that we label people in this way. As a result we try to keep our true feelings a secret but I am sure nearly everybody has been or is prejudice about something or somebody at some point in their lives.

Stereotyping and prejudice together can lead to discrimination. Discrimination happens as a result of our feelings. This is when we treat people differently, badly or unfairly because we have labelled them or placed them in a certain group. We would not give them the time of day or a fair hearing if we discriminated them. If people would only listen to others then it would give the people who have been labelled a chance to change discriminating people's minds.

Throughout my school days I was stereotyped because my dad had a very good Job, worked long hours and very hard, as a result of this we were better off financially than some of my friends at school. My mum did not need to go out to work; my parents had traditional roles. We had family holidays abroad year, sometimes twice a year. My dad had a new car, annually, when the registrations changed and would buy my mum a new car too. At the weekends we would go away to our caravan, where we had a speedboat. This was a way for my dad to unwind from his Job and be able to spend time with his family; we did not see our dad as often as our friends saw their dad's because he worked long hours. We were called posh because of all these things and also because we lived in a big house, I dreaded the kids at school finding out that my dad had a new car or when the caravan season ended and we had the speedboat parked outside the house. When they did find out or see these things they would make comments and my life would be hell at school. When I started High School my dad had bought a plot of land where our new family home was being built, this was an ambition of his and he was fortunate to be able to fulfil his dream.

When the house was finished it was lovely, it had two lounges, five bedrooms, a sauna and a Jacuzzi bath. By the time we moved into the new family home my older brother and sister had passed their driving tests and dad had bought them new cars as a reward for passing first time, as did I when I passed my test. Of course we did not go about bragging about what we had because most people assumed that we were stuck up, my siblings and myself mainly stuck to a group of close friends at school as they did not judge us on the material thing that we had but others often described us as 'That family from the mansion that had everything'. Sometimes it would really annoy myself, my brother and sister when we went out with our friends to the local pub and we would hear people bringing our dad down; saying that he was really stuck up, driving around in his fancy new car with his private registration. All he had ever done was work hard for his family as his own dad had done for him. My dad is now passed retiring age but still works hard everyday, mum and dad now live in another house built for them, they do not have a speedboat but they have swapped the caravan for a cabin on the same site, where they spend weekends relaxing.

It took a while for me to realise that most of the comments and name-calling that we suffered throughout our school years were down to jealousy. Occasionally I still get the same comments about how 'I am from money', now that I am older and wiser it does not bother me as much as it did. I realise that I have been fortunate and all that my parents wanted was the best for their kids and by my dad working hard and my mum looking after us while he did so, my siblings and I had an enjoyable childhood. It was not our fault that our dad was a hard worker and that some of the kids at school were jealous of the way we lived, it was presumed that we were stuck up and posh because they had pre-conceived ideas that wealthy people bragged about what they had. When people got to know us better they realised that we did not think we were better than anyone else and our parents were brought up in hard working families themselves.

If only people who discriminate would let the people that are stereotyped speak then they might learn that things are not always what they seem, resulting in less prejudice in the world. We are all human; we are all born and we all die eventually, the way in which we live our lives in between is what should really matter, not class, race, creed or colour. We should always try not to judge or label but treat others, as we would want to be treated ourselves.

This was the first piece of writing that I had done since I left High School, nearly twenty years before.

I gained a few good friends during my time at college; I still keep in touch with them now even although I was around ten years older than them all. The girls I had become friendly with invited me on a night out; it was the first time I had been out drinking in years. I remember that night so well; we had such a good time although we suffered the following day for it. My sides were sore from laughing so much and my head was killing me from the hangover. I had helped Chloe when she went to the bar to get the drinks that night, whilst we waited she ordered a shot each for us, I asked her if we sipped them and she nearly wet herself laughing then told me to knock it back. I was SO drunk; I ended up getting pushed around in a shopping trolley. I still have the photo's to prove it! The bruises I had the following day! I looked like I had been in a car accident and felt like it too. The drunken chats we had that night; the girls could not help but laugh when I asked them what they meant when they talked about their sex lives, I thought that half of the things they were saying only happened in porn films. They asked me how I managed to get pregnant twice and told me I needed to buy myself a rabbit! It took me a good few days to recover from that night but it did not stop me going back out with them again. I had many a drunken night out with Chloe and Julie, whom I still keep in touch with; they have two kids each, have been married and are now separated from their husbands.

As part of our course work we had to get into small groups and do a presentation to the rest of the class about a nursing establishment that we had visited. Julie, Chloe and I decided to call and ask if we could visit a local hospital for the criminally insane, permission was granted and we went for our day's visit. Many people think of this place as a prison but it is a hospital. We had plenty of questions to ask the staff members and we were given a full tour of the grounds, including some of the locked wards. The patients are free to wander around the grounds; they wear their own clothes, have a gym, pool, garden and small animal enclosure. We enjoyed our day and the presentation went very well when we did it the following week. We even demonstrated how to restrain patients and to use self-defence. Chloe and I were thinking about going into the Mental Health Nursing course at university so we also requested a visit to a hospital for patients with a variety of mental health problems. Ranging from anorexia, self-harming, schizophrenia, dementia to name but a few conditions. Needless to say after both our visits to these establishments we changed our minds and decided to go into General Nursing instead. Maybe the jokes from my sister about Hannibal Lector shouting Clarrise did not help.

During the access to nursing course; Julie, Chloe and I sat together during our science lectures, would laugh about our science tutor, Theo, if you asked him something that he did not have a clear answer for he would just tell us 'it is a given'. We managed to pass all our assessments and to have a great time doing it, we helped each other through the hard times and the year went in very quickly.

When the gala day came to the village that summer I took the kids to the fair along with my brother, sister, her husband and my auntie Pauline. We all had turns on the rides, the kids loved it and never felt ill after being on lots of the rides but Pauline came off from one ride and said she was going to be sick. I told her to go behind one of the large fun fair lorries and be sick there. She says now that I should have know then that nursing was not my vocation.

14

a change for the better

The first time I received my exam results in the post from The Scottish Qualification Awards Board I was so excited and when the kids came in from school that day I was jumping around the kitchen. I kept squeezing their cheeks and asking them 'who has a clever mummy then'. What an ego boost, that was when I realised that I could do anything I put my mind to. Unfortunately after starting my general nursing degree course at university I became unwell, I had to leave after about six months because I had to get a kidney stone removal operation. I was in the hospital for around a week, it was worse than childbirth. After my 'stag horn' kidney stone had been removed I was fitted with a bag to drain the urine from my damaged kidney, to give it time to rest and to repair. I did wonder why there was a safety pin attached to the top of the bag and I soon found out the reason why as I was brushing my teeth the next morning and I had jammed the bag between my stomach and the sink. The bag slipped and jerked the tube that was still inside my kidney, I swear I thought someone had stabbed me in the back; I even looked in to the mirror to see who was behind me. I had to press the call button in the hospital bathroom for help, I lay down after that and the nurse had to examine me to assess any damage, a bit of blood in my urine and a bloody great fright but that was all. The safety pin was to attach the bag to my pyjamas! I wish I had been told that the day before. On the morning I was due to be discharged the nurse explained that they would clamp the tube and that this would restart my kidney; so it would pass urine normally again, it was exceptionally painful when she did this and the clamp had to be taken off again as my kidney had not healed enough to begin working normally on its own. This procedure was tried three times more before I was able to do without the bag and I thought the worst was over as I was told I could go home as soon as they had removed the tube leading from my kidney to the draining bag. There are no words to describe how painful this was, it felt like they were ripping my insides out of my body. I would rather have had breech triplets. Lets hope that never happens again. My poor dad has also had kidney stones but his were small enough to pass, ouch!! When I recovered from that operation I realised that I did not want to become a nurse anymore and started to look into childcare courses; that was always my plan B at the beginning anyway. So at the end of August 2007 I started the HNC in Early Years Education and Childcare Course, again meeting many friends that I still keep in touch with now, one in particular is Jill; she sat across from me in the class. Quiet but funny was my first impression. I would say that the entire class got on well, we helped each other with any difficult assessments and came together well considering our ages ranged from seventeen – forty something.

In January 2008 during a really hard assignment our tutor told the class individually that Jill had been diagnosed with breast cancer, only a few of us knew that she was being tested. It was so sad, all we could think about was he three young boys. Jill had to go through a double mastectomy and chemotherapy as she was told that she had a very aggressive form of breast cancer. We took it in turns to go and visit her in the hospital, I remember taking her in a big bag of her favourite chocolates, which was bad as she is also a diabetic; I just wanted her to smile during this awful time! Jill lost her hair, was in a lot of pain and felt awful but still managed to look after her three small boys, attend college, hand in her course work on time and keep smiling. There are no words to describe just how brave she was during that hard and scary time of her life. On the advise of her doctors Jill had her ovaries removed as a prevention and also had reconstructive breast surgery, she has had four years cancer free now and I really hope that she does not have to go through anything like that ever again. I visited her after her surgeries and could not believe how upbeat she always was, a true inspiration. She had massive stepping stones of her own to get over then, but she managed. At the end of my HNC course the college held a graduation ceremony, I was so nervous, I spent ages the day before selecting my outfit and giving myself a manicure. I had a dream the night before the ceremony that I fell, tripping over my graduation gown when my name was called for me to go up on to the stage to collect my certificate. My mum, dad, Marianne and my daughter were there to see the ceremony, they were all extremely proud of me and I was on a high, I could not believe how far I had come, I never imagined that I would have a graduation gown on or be awarded with a certificate. I really wanted to keep the gown and take it home but you had to return it as it was only hired for the day and also to get your own jacket back, I imagined wearing it around the house! I think back to how difficult it was at times to do the assignments and essays on time when I had a house and two kids to look after, I would definitely recommend that people should try to gain a good quality of education while they are young, while they have no ties or anything holding them back, like a nasty ex husband.

During the graduation Jill was given a special award, all of her classmates were extremely proud of her. Jill visits me at home when I feel unwell, usually bringing her yummy homemade cupcakes and we have also met up with not only the tutors from the course but also some of the other girls. Again we all keep in touch on Facebook.

Before we were permitted to worked at our three placements as part of the course we had to pass the Health and Hygiene course as we would be preparing and serving the children with snacks, we also had to get a police background check called a 'Disclosure Scotland' because we would be working and looking after vulnerable people, i.e. young children.

In 2002 the janitor at a primary school in Soham, England, murdered two ten-year-old girls. This man had previously been arrested but not charged with a variety of sexual offences, including sex with a minor, rape and attempted rape. Because he had not been charge with any of these offences then his name did not appear on any police records. Disclosure Scotland carries out a background check prior any individual being permitted to work within areas where there are vulnerable people but if that person has not been charged with a crime it will not show up and may result in someone else harming a defenceless child or vulnerable adult. I personally feel that the laws need to tighten up to ensure the safety of all concerned. More thorough checks must be carried out, if they were then this janitor would not have been given a job within a primary school and these two young girls would have been safe and still alive.

For the first and the third placement I worked for six weeks at the local nursery; attached to the primary school, where Caroline worked. Not only did I go to that primary school, my own kids also attended the nursery and then the primary school, it is about three minutes walk from my house. I more than loved it, in fact I even went on my college days off and helped when the old nursery was knocked down (primary two class when I attended that school) and we moved all the equipment, old and new to a purpose built nursery attached onto the other side of the school. It is so rewarding to watch a young child grow in confidence and knowledge and having the privilege to be part of assisting them. Most people think all you do is play with the kids but that is how they learn at that age. The other placement was within a primary two class at the school in the next village, I hated every single day of the six weeks. It was far too quiet compared to the nursery settings; the children aged six or seven just sat all day, working, no play involved within their learning. During each placement the course tutor visits you to assess how you are getting along and also to observe you with a small group of the children doing an activity. After another year at college I graduated as a fully qualified childcare practitioner/nursery nurse. I actually got paid for being a big kid and playing with toys. I loved it! Glutton for punishment I went back to college for night classes to do an additional course within early years childcare. I feel that I am all studied out but never say never.

Straight after college I became employed by a small company who provided mobile crèches, we would go to various locations and set up playrooms and activities for children of various ages. We would either meet with the manager who had all the toys, activities etc in the van or a staff member would drive the van. I took my turn driving. I loved working with the small babies, which was my favourite part of this job. The staff members got on well and we had many laughs together and with the children. We set up a game of under five's skittles, where the kids stood facing away from us on a bench where a large crash mat was place directly in front of them. We would take turns at knocking them off of the bench on to the mat by bouncing a large gym ball towards them. I am not sure if the staff or the kids laughed the most. The Job was about making the kids time within the crèche enjoyable and we tried our best at all times. During my time with this company I went on a Child Protection Course and also a First Aid course for adults, children or small infants. I hoped that I would not need to use the skills that I had learnt during these courses. Unfortunately I was wrong. I left this company as the crèches were not in high demand and started to work as a supply nursery nurse within the nurseries of a variety of local primary schools. I was getting more money and more shifts. One day while I was helping a little girl get changed in to her nursery inside shoes I commented on how nice her t shirt was, I told her that it was pretty and she said 'yes, it is new. **** gave it to me because I did not tell mummy', I could feel my stomach churn but I just kept putting her shoes on for her; then she told me ' I do not like what he does, he hurts me and it is sore'. It was my worst nightmare come true. I lifted her off of the bench and told her to go in to the nursery to join her friends. I had to take what this gorgeous little 3-year-old blond girl had told me straight to the head teacher, who in turn called Social Services and the Police. It was out of my hands now and I never did find out what happened after that, it was considered confidential even although she had brought it to my attention first. It turns my stomach to think about what this little girl had gone through. I do know that it was not the new step dad as he came along with the little girls mum to collect her at home time. This would not have been permitted if it had been him.

15

trying again

I decided that for my daughter's birthday that year that we would have a small party at home, we invited all my family, the kid's friends and some of the neighbours. We all enjoyed the games and the more alcohol that the adults consumed the sillier the games became. We played at who could eat the most small cakes the quickest, hide and seek inside the house and we had a length of string that we passed from one person to the next, the point of this games was to feed the string up or down inside your clothes then pass it on for the next person to do the same; everyone ended up joined together. Some people had string burns after this game. When most of the people had left and when it was dark we played cards with my two kids, the only adults that were left over were myself, my sister and her sister in law. We decided to open another bottle of wine and order a Chinese meal, the only problem was that I did not have a bottle opener and Lyndsay sent my kids next door to ask if we could borrow their one. The kids went next door in their pyjamas so that we could have more wine!

Not long after the party I began to notice that my left eye was showing signs of the Iritis again; I went to the ear, nose and throat department of my local hospital, where funnily enough they also treat eyes! I was given the numbing drops and then the injection into my eyeball again, I think Marianne was going to be sick as she watched, she drove me there and back as I had an eye patch on after the injection. Just like a pirate! On our way back home we went to John's work and waited until it was his break time so that I could tell him what had happened, he came out to the car and we talked for ten minutes, it sort of made me feel better. I had steroid drops to use again and had to attend a further few appointment until my eye became better. The only problem was that the infection damage my pupil in my left eye, it had blown which means that it does not open or dilate at all, it remains the same size all the time.

This looks kind of strange as the right eye's pupil works perfectly so they can appear very different, it only get on my nerves when it is very sunny. People do not usually notice but sometime I can feel them looking at me just that little bit longer. That is when I tell them that my eye was damaged due to an infection and the pupil will not recover now. I was more gutted that it happened twenty years after the first time it took place, this meant that I was older and I did not feel twenty years older. Kids usually notice it and ask why I have a big eye! I still manage to wear my contact lenses and have my glasses for when my eyes get tired. I would need a guide dog for the blind if I did not use either my glasses or lenses.

It took me around four years before I thought I was ready to even try having a relationship again. My mum kept telling me that she did not like the way I sat in the house every single night, that I should be getting taken out and shown off. I was quite happy with my own company. A friend advised me that it was much easier to join an on line-dating site, which I did and I met three very different men. Batchelor number one was a cocky 'B' who talked me out of £450 and made me feel like I was losing my confidence again, especially when he commented on how I looked dressed and undressed or how I was not correct about something but he always was, although he promised me that he would repay me the money; I am still waiting; I think I will just need to write it off as being soft and stupid. Bachelor number two was a very thin man and so quiet, to the extent that it was very awkward when someone else was in our company, he lacked any enthusiasm for life but proposed and I accepted, I can only say that I was blinded by the sparkly diamonds and enjoyed the fact that he wanted me. It is nice to feel needed but he was more than boring and it ended up exasperating me that he could not hold a conversation with anyone, even with me, it was exhausting. He was shocked when I broke off the engagement. Hindsight is a great thing! I went from one extreme to the other, a very thin man who never spoke, to a very large man who never shut up. Introducing bachelor number three, he started off ok, he was full of the charm, knew exactly what to say, made me laugh but it turned out that he was charming other girls too. His snoring was so loud that you would think that a truck was revving up next to your head while you tried to sleep, even with earplugs. At times when I could not listen to it anymore I would wake him and I would be told to F off and sleep somewhere else. 'In my own house'. He also told me that the perfume I wore every day smelt like cats piss! Charming, it did not put him off in the beginning, I nearly had to beat him off and anyway I was not going to change my perfume for him; my granny had bought that scent as a Christmas present when I was fourteen and I have been wearing it everyday since and have no intentions of changing that. I did know that he was a bit of a player before I got with him but I stupidly thought that he had calmed down after being with me for nearly a year, I was dumped two days after my birthday. The only good thing that came out of being involved with bachelor number three is that I now have a very good friend in his cousin's wife, Louise, and we meet as often as we can to have a catch up. All I can say is that I was treated like a mug and I allowed it to happen, you really do not live and learn with age. Louise and I laugh about it all now.

16

enjoying being single

I always made sure that my kids had their eyes tested every two years, went to their dental check ups every six months and I took them to the doctor if they were ill. I know that they do not do theses things now. I always tried my best to make our lives fun as we had been miserable before. You do not need money to have fun. Although I did buy the kids a fifteen-foot trampoline that they used daily, Marianne and I used it at the weekends when they were at their dad's. We were bouncing on it after a couple of 'lemonades' one sunny day and ended up playing at topless trampolining; my daughter came back to the house as she had forgotten something and decided that it was much better fun if she stayed with Marianne and I on the trampoline.

I was so proud of her for standing up to her dad and telling him that she was not going back to his house that day. Some of the other silly stuff I got up to with my own kids; we would played the left and right game in the car, taking it in turns when we got to junctions and ending up lost mostly, we went to see all the kids films and wore the panda masks all through Kung Foo Panda, we played chap door run, drew all over the outside house walls with chalk, but the best night that we had was when after a few glasses of 'lemonade' Marianne, myself and the kids went out dressed in strange outfits; I had my housecoat on and Marianne borrowed my sons clothes. We played at chap door run then we went to the nearby swing park, when I went down the slide and hit my head off of the end, we was decided that we should go to my mum and dad's house to have a seat. My mum ended up making Marianne and myself sandwiches and strong coffee, sobering us up before sending us home. When the kids were really small I remember having fun with them as I drew paws on their toes with a biro, which made prints on the laminate floor in the lounge, we also drew tattoos on each other and the kids drew moustaches on themselves and pretended to be one of their uncle's. Daddy would not have approve. I would also put different items on the living room table; like the remote control, an ornament, a pen or keys, let the kids take a look then take one away when they had turned their backs, a sort of memory game. The things you do when the television is not very good! We would also watch their films and have a competition to see who could eat the most crisps during the film. I can only hope that the kids will remember all the laughs we had and the times we all laughed until we cried.

I did not feel confident enough or have the money to afford to go abroad with the kids on my own but two years running we went to two different caravan parks on the Scottish Borders. The kids had a brilliant time, what with all the amusements, the swimming pool activities and the horse riding, dancing, football, golf buggies and multi person bike hire. It would probably have been cheaper if we had went abroad but it was worth every penny to see them so happy. We also went to the Dominican Republic with my mum and dad for two weeks, as a treat. We flew from Manchester Airport, I am a nervous flyer, I was taking herbal remedies and white wine but still ended up getting dragged on to the plane by my mum, the last passenger, with tears and snot, not a very attractive look. We pretended to the kids that granny and granda were going to London and that the plane would land again not long after take off, they were not long in clicking that was not the truth when they saw the small aeroplane bleeping on the screen going across the water. I wished that the aircraft did not have that, as watching all the water we were crossing made me extremely nervous, I cried for most of the flight. We were all inclusive in a very posh hotel complex just off of the beach. It as not safe to go outside of the complex, we had no need to as we had everything that we needed, it was paradise. However, there was no mobile phone signal at all within the complex; it took me the entire first week to get over my text addiction, I always have my mobile beside me. When we went out for the day on an excursion all you could heard on the coach were peoples mobile phones bleeping with text messages, I think Marianne and John thought I had fallen out with them as I usually text them lots daily. On our days excursion we swam with the dolphins; well my son and I did, as my daughter was a bit scared, she was only eight at the time. My mum and dad did not want to do it either; my mum had the job of videoing our experience and dad looked after my daughter. The two dolphin trainers gave the group our life jackets, the instructions on what was going to happen and what we were supposed to do. My son went first out of the small group, the two dolphins swam out and he had to stretch out both of his arms and grab the dolphin's dorsal fins as they passed. The first time they swam straight passed him, as he did not put his arms out far enough and the dolphins were very quick. When it came to my turn I grabbed the fins but as we were rushing through the water; holding on, the dolphin on my left side hit my thigh with its flipper, it was so painful but I could not let go, plus my bikini bottoms were slipping off. By the time I got to the pool steps I was struggling to climb them because of my sore leg and I was also trying to pull my bikini bottoms up before my mum caught my bare ass on film. The bruise I had covered my thigh and made me limp for the week. Not very attractive. To top it all off I got a splinter in my foot from the jetty and my son had to help me to the first aid hut, they stood scratching their heads for about five minutes then they were appalled when I asked for a needle to remove it myself. After that fiasco my son and I joined my mum and dad to watch the younger kids and the older people in a small pool where a dolphin would cuddle and kiss them, my daughter loved it. After visiting the dolphins we went to see the tigers, they had orange and black tigers and also the white and black type. The tourists were permitted to feed the tigers through a small hole cut out of the glass in their enclosure. The raw meat was put on to a large fork, which was attached to a round piece of Perspex then you put it through the hole to feed the tiger. We have some amazing photos of this holiday, it is something I will always treasure and never forget. It really was a treat from my parents. I probably will never have the opportunity to be able to afford to go back to a place as beautiful. What a great experience.

17

losing my son

Three days before mother's day in 2007 after various problems, my son had a temper tantrum (again) and walked out of the house, he went to his dads and did not come home. I was scared that day as he had grabbed me by the wrists and threatened to hit me if I did not let him go, I had no choice, but after speaking to his dad I was relieved that he said he was going to bring our son back after he had cooled down the next day, he also said that he could not stay with him and that he had told him he had to come home to live with me. That never happened; in fact it only got worse, my own son smashed my windows, broke into my shed and some items were stolen. I also had threats by texts and phone calls from his dad mainly but also from my son, to the extent that I had to involve the police. I put all of his things in several large bags and left them outside my back door, inside the garden gate, it was a dry day. I kept the door locked as I was scared of what he would do when he came to collect them, especially if his dad was with him. He told anyone who would listen that I had thrown all of his things around the garden. Another lie. My son never did come back to live with me, he did not even visit me; in fact he has not been in my house since the day he left.

I can only hope that when he grows up he will realise the truth and how much I love him, I always will.

It really upsets me that this happened after everything I did for him, I stood by him whenever he was in trouble at the school and especially when he committed a horrendous crime with his friend. They had stolen two small pet rabbits out of someone's back garden, put them in a cage and then they placed the ferret that my son had as a pet in beside the rabbits. I did not see the aftermath but I am sure that you can imagine what happened to the rabbits, I was lucky that I did not witness or hear about what the ferret did to those poor defenceless rabbits. When I heard about this from a neighbour I was shocked and sickened. They had been bragging about what they had done at school and of course word gets back. I advised my son that it would be in his own best interest to hand himself in to the police as they would be coming to see him when they had heard about what had happened. We went to the police station that night, I was so upset, and I never imagined having to sit beside my son as he gave a statement to a police officer. Throughout the process my son lied and was quite nasty to the police officer, even when he was cuffed and taken to another station where his fingerprints, photograph and DNA would be taken he still kept up the lies. When the police officer asked him what he thought about how upset his mum was, he said he 'did not even care'. The result of this crime was that he was given a caution by the police, the Scottish Society for the Prevention of Cruelty to Animals took his ferret away from him , I was advised not to allow him to have any more pets and not to leave him in the same room as my cat or they would need to take her away too. The minute he moved in with his dad he was allowed a dog and some more ferrets.

It was a very stressful time, not just for me but for my daughter too as she knew her brother had broken my windows and she had heard about the ferret incident. She was threatened with violence from her own brother if she told me the truth. The last thing I ever wanted was my son to live with his dad, I knew that he would not have many rules there and as it turned out he was allowed to smoke, take drugs, drink and have underage sex. I had high hopes for him as he was very academic, he wanted to go to university and to study to become an architect, at the moment he is working in a tyre and exhaust outlet, has his own flat now but I have not seen him since I gave him his bank account passbook on his eighteenth birthday. I am glad that he has a job and his own flat now; I only wished that he visited. It is very sad and upsets me but he is all the man he will ever be at eighteen, an adult with his own mind. He has proved just what I thought he was going to do by only coming for his money on his birthday, as he has not visiting me or any of my side of the family since.

18

stumbling while sober

In June 2007 I had an operation on my left kneecap, seemingly I had damaged it by over-doing it at the gym and it needed 'scraped'. I admit that I did do too much at the gym, my dad used to laugh about this as I asked him for a note to get out of doing physical education at school every week. Knowing what I know now I would not have bothered with the operation, it made my knee a million times worse instead of any better. It was not very reassuring at the time when the doctor kept asking me which leg it was over and over just before I was given my pre med.

While I was in the hospital having my knee operated on I had a decorator wallpapering my stairs, hall and my landing. Marianne and I had stripped the old wallpaper off the week before the decorator was due to come. Anyway, I was pleased with the end result, it brightened up my house. I had one roll of wallpaper to take back to the do it yourself store. Marianne took me as I was unable to drive and we borrowed an electric scooter from the main entrance of the store because there was no way that I could manage to walk around the huge store. What a laugh we had with the scooter, Marianne jumped on to the back, I was whizzing around and while I was reversing I accidentally knocked in to there cushion display; toppling them over. I am glad that it was not a paint display I had bumped into; imagine the mess. We could not talk for laughing.

My daughter, Marianne and I went to Benidorm just for a week in the sun and for me to chill out after my operation. It was a week of self-catering in a 'hotel', not the nicest of places I have been to. Chill, good grief it was like trying to keep the peace between two moody teenagers, so not exactly the chill out week I had hoped or planned for. One day as we were playing in the pool with a ball, it went out on to the poolside so I got out to retrieve it as I was closest and fell over nothing, blaming it on my knee healing. I would know the real reason why I fell over within a matter of months. My daughter had a real strop mid week when she refused to come to the pool in her swimming suit, I had had enough by then so I just left her to come down dressed in her denim shorts and her t-shirt. I think it took less than an hour of scorching sunshine before she gave in and asked for the apartment key so that she could get changed, what a mood she was in on that day, she did not want to put on sun cream and this resulted in her shoulders being burnt. Teenagers think that they know everything! I insisted that she wear a t shirt when she was swimming or playing in the pool for the rest of the week and also when she was sitting sunning herself I got her to drape the wet t shirt around her shoulders to protect them and to stop then from becoming any worse.

Anyway not long after the Benidorm holiday I started to stumble when I was doing random things in the house; I just put it down to my knee recovering from being scrapped, but when I mentioned it to my doctor at my check up, she advised me to note down every time I had a stumble and what I was doing at the time. When I took my list back a week later she told me that it did not sound like it was anything to do with my kneecap and she recommended that I see a neurologist. I think I sat in her room dumb struck as she told me that she would write a referral letter to the local hospital. I was really upset, I wanted to see John, he always made everything better when he spoke to me or gave me a hug but we had not spoken since bachelor number three told me that I could not have a man as a friend when I was seeing him. I was imagining all sorts of things so I went straight to my mum and dad's house where I told them about how worried I was about my health. I had not mentioned the stumbling to them as I thought it was just my knee healing. As parents do, they said that everything would be ok and not to worry. I have got to be honest and say that I thought I had a brain tumour or something scary like that so when my mum and dad offered to pay for me to go private instead of waiting for my NHS appointment, I was so very grateful. My doctor organised it and I had my first appointment with the private neurologist a week later in Edinburgh, he examined me, asked me to walk, balance on one foot and then while I was laying on the table with my eyes closed, he prodded my feet with a pin and asked me to let him know when or if I felt it. I burst into tears then, I had been so worried all week but when he was doing this and I did not feel the pin at all I got so upset and frightened. I was really scared and then I felt awful when the doctor apologised for making me upset. I had been holding those tears in all day. A Magnetic Resonance Imaging Scan, an M.R.I was the next step to finding out what was happening; so a week after being examined by the neurologist I spent around 50 minutes inside a tunnel with music playing in the headphones to try (unsuccessfully) to drown out the deafening drilling noises, how ironic that I was listening to Coldplay sing 'If I lay here', I will never listen to that song in the same way again. I was given the computer disk with my scan information on it to take home with me, so when I got in to the house I put it straight into the laptop. My brain looks like I have two large round white earrings just above where my ears are, other than that I could not see anything else that looked different, of course I did not know what I was looking for. I was fascinated looking at my body in such detail, all my organs and bones in perfect detail. Anyway, five days after my M.R.I scan experience I received a letter from the private neurologist, explaining his diagnosis to me in Latin so I did what everybody does now and typed the words into Google but I did not believe what it came up with so I went back to see my own doctor, the one who had referred me in the first place. After asking me what I thought the words meant she confirmed that I indeed did had Relapsing Remitting Multiple Sclerosis. I did not and would not believe her, I was just a bit off balance; people who had MS are in wheelchairs and need carers.

There was only one person I wanted to talk to when I got back in to the car after being diagnosed with this disease, but John and I had not spoken for nearly a year now. I no longer had his number stored on my mobile phone. How I wished I could just call his number, he would know what to say to me, he always did make me feel better about everything. I could not go to my own house and sit, alone, numb with worry and confusion so I went to my parents house; I think they were shocked like myself but also relieve it was not something life threatening. My mum said that maybe it was a mistake and dad said that we should get a second opinion. I just could not take anything in, I felt like I had been told I was going to die.

Now for the science bit, sorry to bore you but this is the MS jargon that patient's get told straight after their diagnosis! Something that you do not take in and is not much use to you anyway, all you want to know is how to get on with your daily life. All the important questions like; - When did I get this? , How did it happen? Why me? Or What will happen to me now? These questions are answered with 'I do not know' by the neurologists, the so-called experts. The experts are the people who have MS. I have many friends on Facebook, we have a few support groups, we talk often and we all discuss the above questions or any new signs or symptoms that we are experiencing; I have never heard 'I do not know' from any one of them.

Multiple Sclerosis is an auto immune system disease, which attacks the fatty myelin insulating sheath that covers the long fibres called axons in the nerve cells within the brain and the spinal cord; (the CNS or Central Nervous System), resulting in nerve damage. The nerves cells in the brain and spinal cord are unable to communicate or send messages by the usual electrical signal. (I would describe it as a short circuit) This disease affects more women than men and patients usually live in colder climates. At the moment there is no cure but research continues so maybe one day there will be a cure. MS will not kill you but you may die as a result of you immune system being unable to fight off an infection or illness. People with MS have a life span; on average of 7 years shorter than that of a person who does not have MS.

I sat in silence when I went back for my final consultation with the private neurologist a week later; the only things that I wanted to know were if I could pass this condition on to my kids and if the doctor though it was MS when he first examined me, he said he did and no I could not pass it on to my kids. When I got back to my parents house I was crying because I had not said thanks to the neurologist; my dad told me that he did it for me when he paid his bill! At least it made me laugh. Trust my dad to make me laugh when I felt my whole world was closing in on me.

I told all of my immediate family first about my diagnosis, I think they were all knocked for six, the same as I was. Then I told my friends, Marianne and Shannon cried and I did not know how to react to this, I felt like they were behaving as if

I was going to die. At that time I was not even sure myself if I was going to die or not, I had been told the MS jargon but I did not really know what it was that was wrong with me apart from the two letters that shorten the diseases name. I still get 'I am so sorry' whenever I tell people about my illness, people do not know how to react.

I went a bit over the top after my diagnosis, I got my long hair cut short as I thought I would not be able to look after it by myself, it is growing back now and something I regret doing at the time. I nearly told the company I worked for that I would not be able to carry on at my job within the nurseries. I cried and cried, I was in total denial though, I kept saying 'I do not have MS, and there is nothing wrong with me'. Oh and I got another three symbol tattoos on my left forearm, one meaning courage, one meaning hope and the other meaning infinity.

I did not have time to let the diagnosis sink in before I had my first major relapse; just six weeks after being diagnosed I started to feel a tingling sensation in my left leg, which travelled up to waist high (only on the left side) then stopped. I saw my MS nurse for the first time on the Tuesday and by the Friday I was dragging my left leg. By that time I needed crutches to get about the house, I would not go out at all because I thought people would be looking at me. I had to use a commode during the day, I had accidents and I was mortified with myself. I had to get my daughter to help me dress and undress, as I could not lift my left leg at all. I was referred to a Hospital in Edinburgh where they deal with MS, I was given steroids to stop my relapse getting worst but the neurologist there explained that was all they could really do for me and that the relapse would take its own time to get better. I may never make a full recovery though. Travelling back home that day I was not in the right frame of mind and ended up getting a speeding ticket, £60 fine and three points on my licence. I am just surprised that it was my first speeding fine as I admit I always drive way too fast and always have done since I passed my driving test at seventeen. I just did not care that day, the last thing that I was thinking about was how fast I was driving. I could have appealed against the fine but it was the last thing on my mind.

I have had depression before but I have never felt as low as I did right then. Eventually, two months later and after I had gotten over the relapse the neurologist prescribed a drug treatment, which involved me having to inject myself three times a week. A disease modifying drug, DMD's that are designed to reduce relapse rates. The experts are not completely sure if these drugs work as they should and after asking I was told that the only way of testing them is to stop taking them altogether and risk relapsing. No thanks!

I get my injection medication delivered to my house every month. It comes in an unmarked white van and it always makes me laugh, the cardboard box that my medication is stored in is also delivered in an unmarked box. The driver even covers up the yellow sharps bin so that nobody sees it. All of my neighbours know about my condition; the driver once told me that sometimes neighbours and even patients partners do not know that the person has MS. You would think that they would notice. Each to there own!

I have lost count of the amount of times I have had a stumble, slipped and fell due to my balance issues, I have fallen down the stairs often but getting in and out of the bath to have a shower were the worse times. I have giving myself some very nice bruises and black eyes. Luckily I have not broken anything, not yet anyway. I eventually got a wet floor shower room installed and since then I have not had as many falls. It took just over a week to be installed but it was so worth it, the first couple of days when I used it I felt as if I was staying in one of the Hilton hotels. I also have a stair lift which I now use each time I go up and down the stairs. I have learnt the hard way. I have an alarm system within the house, I wear the button pendant all the time and I can press for help at anytime; Marianne, my dad, my auntie, my sister and my next door neighbour have keys and the alarm company would call them to assist me if I needed it. There is also a sensor within the alarms that picks up on my movements around the house; if I did not move around then they would buzz me and ask if I was ok, the sensor signal is turned off between 10pm and 7am. There are railings at the back door to assist me in getting up and down the steps and paving slabs to make it easier if I am using my wheelchair. I am such a determined person, I have been told that this helps me fight my MS and that because I was very fit before my diagnosis that I am not as disabled as I could have been. I just know that I will not let it beat me! I just get up from a fall and laugh at myself; I really need a stunt double!

I find myself looking at photos or recalling times in the past where I have fallen and wondered if I had MS then, I had, and still do have so many questions but sadly they will remain unanswered, as even the specialists 'do not know', that is what they say when you ask them a question and I always have questions for them. MS affects individuals differently and it is a case of just taking one day at a time, that is what I do now, I judge how good my day is going to be from when I get out of my bed and if I can walk over to the window and open my curtains. The only thing I can say about having MS is that 'if you do not have it then you do not get it!!!! Trying to explain feelings and thoughts to someone who does not have it is pointless and frustrating. A healthy person does not understand you when you talk about your leg having toothache!

Some people who have MS have had stem cells from a baby's umbilical cord injected in to their spine, one story I read stated that it is a miracle cure as the woman got out of her wheelchair and walked for the first time in sixteen years and other story I read; the patient was left paralysed, had fingers and toes amputated and then she died. Another experimental treatment involves cutting in to the base of your brain to correct the constricted veins allowing the blood to flow freer. I have not read up on this as the thought of someone cutting in to my neck or brain gives me the shivers. Neurologists do not recommend either of theses experimental treatments so it is a case of just keep on taking the injections until the research comes up with a proven cure. Many people with MS think there wont be a cure in the near future as the drug companies make too much money out of the drugs they sell.

Although MS is not life threatening I decided that I wanted to get my will in order and after doing so I felt a huge weight off of my shoulders as if I was settled now. I told my family that I had done this and that if my MS got to the stage where I was not enjoying the quality of my life then I would end it myself. I had no choice about the MS starting but I could choose when it was going to end. My parents were worried about me because I had done this until I explained to them that it could be many years before I felt the need to do this, I just wanted my feelings made clear. My sister, without my knowledge called my GP and also my MS nurse and told them that she though I was unstable, as a result, the MS nurse visited my house and explained a few things about MS to my sister and parents. I was really annoyed that this had happened and my mum hung back when they were leaving the house, telling me that she was worried it was going to cause a family rift. I am not sure who said this but my mum told me that a family member said that I would be sectioned under the mental health act and that I would get my daughter taken away from me. My granny used to say that there is nothing funnier that folk! I was very hurt at the time and I wished that my sister had spoken to me first. I could have explained how I felt about things. It was good of my MS nurse to come out to my house and she did explain the condition to my sister and my parents.

19

living with ms

In the January 2010; after being told I had MS I went back to my favourite nursery to work, I was very nervous about my ability to do my job and if I had been going to a new setting I do not think that I would have managed it. The entire school staff were brilliant, they helped me regain my confidence; it probably helped that I knew the kids and had already worked with them for over a year and unbeknown to them and myself I would continue to work with them for a further two years. I still continued to enjoy the nursery day trips out to the zoo or to the theatre, the only thing I did not enjoy was when the Zoo Lab came to the school and visited the nursery with their spiders, cockroaches and those reptiles I hate! I had to ask to swap with another staff member from the school so that I was not in the nursery while the children enjoyed being told about these animals or were permitted to hold them I actually preferred to do paperwork than to be in the same room as those creatures!

The nursery staff got on so well, it was not like going to work, we had nights out, typed up cheeky school reports for each other;

it felt more like friends who looking after children during the day, that was until we had all the paperwork to fill in, the kids school reports and the parents appointments. These tasks were mainly done in our own time. That made it more like work, we were united on the fact that the paperwork took the focus off of the children's learning through their play and that we should let them enjoy their two years at the nursery, saving the paperwork and the more structured routine for when they started primary school.

It also helped that I had and still do have a fantastic team of professionals to assist me, an occupational therapist, a physiotherapist, a psychologist. These people are just a phone call away and are willing to do anything that they can to help me, which is wonderful. I do know of other people who have MS who are not as lucky; one friend in particular has been discharged from her neurologist, I find this strange as there is no cure so why has she been discharged as she will need the neurologist at some point. At work I was 'me', the nursery nurse with the sense of humour and the cheeky smile, but at home I was a wreck, crying all the time, zero confidence, panic attacks at the thought of going out, I remember being invited for a night out to celebrate a friends birthday, I just could not make myself go, I felt sick, I was shaking and crying. My psychologist came weekly to the house to just talk about things and to help me regain some of my confidence; she helped me to realise that when I was outside of the house people would not be looking at me being off balance or using my crutches or stick as they are busy with their own thoughts and tasks. I was so paranoid about people looking at me; judging me. I got in touch with a local MS group, found out the times of the meetings and really had to force myself to go, I knew that I needed to do it, I felt sick at the though of going but I was so glad that I did make that first step. I met a few people who understood how it felt to have MS, who understood what it felt like to have toothache in your arm or leg! I also met a lovely couple, James (a clinical psychologist) and Karen, his lovely wife, whom I now regard as very close friends. I went to the fortnightly group meetings for about a year, I helped with many fund raising activities, attended the Christmas night out but decided to stop going when James told me that he had been treated very badly by the chairperson of the group. That made me so mad as James was helping the group in his own time and never ever said no; in fact he went above and beyond to help the group. Nobody gets away with being nasty to my friends! It was also alleged that money, which had been raised by the group had disappeared, that ended it for me. I did not want to be associated with the group after that.

James advised me to attend a place called The Little Haven for various therapies, counselling from James initially and also some exercise sessions to build up my muscles and my core strength. My sessions with James lasted a good few months and helped me overcome many hurdles in my life. If it was not for James I would not have started writing this, he advised me to write down all of the good things that have happened in my life and I sort of got carried away! I attended The Little Haven weekly for exercises for over a year, I call Sharon, the instructor 'Hitler' jokingly as she works me really hard; she also gave me exercise homework! I still do the exercises that she showed me at home now; I want to keep being as strong as I possibly can for as long as I can. I keep in touch with James and Karen; I am very fond of them. We keep in touch by email and I also visiting them, seemingly I am welcome anytime. Maybe they will regret saying that when I turn up with a suitcase and a smile!

My daughter and I were sitting in the house one Friday night; we were extremely bored, the television was rubbish and we were trying to make up our minds on what we could do to alleviate our boredom. A spur of the moment decision to go to the local large grocery store lightened my purse as usual 'madam' got what she wanted! When we came to the end of one of the shopping isles, my daughter said 'is that not that man you used to work with', I bumped straight in to John, after a year of no contact at all; I could not believe it. The very person I had really needed to talk to was right in front of me. I must have looked a real state, still in my nursery working clothes; my hair tied back, white faced with lack of sleep and through endless crying. We stopped and said hello, how are you doing, that sort of thing; general chatting and then he asked me why I had a stick; what had I been doing to myself. When I told him I had been diagnosed with MS his face went as white as mine. Our conversation did not last long after that, then he said that he was sorry to hear about my diagnosis and said he betters get on with his shopping. As he walked away I could tell that he had wanted to say something else to me so I stopped him and asked him what was wrong but he just said that it was ok. When I got home I could have kicked myself for not asking for his mobile number again or asking him if he still had mine as I wanted to have a proper conversation with him. If I had know that I was going to bump in to him after all this time I would have made an effort, not still have been wearing my paint and snot encrusted working clothes.

Marianne visited the next day and we came up with a plan. We would go down to his house and slip a note with my phone number through the letterbox. So off we went but when we got closer to the house we realised that it was the local gala day, the entire village was busy with people, we sat in the car for ages and debated what to do as I was not sure if I was doing the right thing or not. Maybe he did not want to get back in touch with me, especially now that I had MS. Marianne told me straight that he was not a shallow man and that there was no way that he would think of me any differently, if I did nothing I was wasting a chance as it could be another year before I saw him again.

Nothing like a reality check! That did it for me; we ended up walking through the gala day park; where the children's races were being held. Suddenly across the field I spotted him, sitting beside the rest of his family; I could not believe it, he looked so good. Marianne persuaded me to go around for a closer look, just as we were about to move he had a big stretch putting both of his hands behind his head, Marianne and I both sighed like two teenagers then burst out laughing. I still had the same feelings for him as I did before we had lost contact, I had to do something or I would regret it. When we got closer Marianne suddenly said that they were on the move and that we had better get back to her car quickly, I cannot do quickly but I did my best. We just got in to the car and John walked past carrying the chairs that he and his family had been sitting on, Marianne shouted his name, he stopped; looking surprised to see us and I blurted out 'do you still have my number and can you call me as I really need to talk to you'. He said yes he would call and I told him that we had to go now. I was a gibbering wreck on the way back to my house, had I done the right thing?

John called me the very next morning and we arranged for him to visit so that we could have that talk. That was nearly a couple of years ago now, we have talked plenty, he has visited lots, we have had days and nights out together. We have been out for the day in the car and have also been for meals out, as well as me cooking for us at my house. We are back to texting lots and lots, calling and enjoying each other's company. It would be nice if we could get together as we get on so well, who knows what is ahead of us.

I was never one for reading as a child but during my thirties I have read every type of book I can get my hands on, one thing I have noticed is that the majority of books I have read have happy endings, the couples always get together eventually, their sex life is brilliant, nobody has any long term illnesses, they have beautiful children and fantastic jobs. Really annoying, entertaining but definitely not real life! I laughed with a friend at the romantic novels where it takes ten chapters until the couple finally kiss, the looks, yearning, lusting and the glances; all I wanted to do, whilst reading them was shout 'just grab him'. I have to be honest, I am not really sure how it came about but I was invited to join a group of women's amateur erotic fiction writers on Facebook, which I did. This lead to me writing around ten fictional erotic short stories and I am proud to say I got one published in an on line women's magazine. I did write a couple of stories for two of my friends, changing their names of course. Protecting their innocence! Maybe not the sort of gift for a friend but they liked them and seemingly I was not far off the truth, I must know them better than they thought. Anyway back to some cleaner writing!

During my first annual check up with my neurologist; your neurologist only sees you annually. I was persuaded to change my injections to another type of disease modifying drugs, mainly because it was £200 cheaper per month for the NHS. This type involves me preparing the drugs and syringes myself; I had to inject every other day instead of three times a week. I still get headaches around an hour after doing my injections and the site marks look like big bruises.

When I think about those first couple of months when I had to do my own injections; how I would burst into tears whenever I saw the yellow sharps box, now just over 3 years since my very first injection. I still inject to reduce my relapses and I do it without even blinking now; It is just something I do automatically, like getting dressed or brushing my hair. No big deal.

20

losing my daughter

Sadly in January 2011 my daughter at the age of thirteen decided that she would rather live with her dad; it was upsetting enough that she wanted to do this but when she told lies to her dad, step mum and then a social worker which were ridiculous and could have cost me my job at that time. She alleged that I hit her, got drunk and had men in the house frequently. Good grief, if only I had the energy and both of my kids were bigger that me by the time they were ten years old. The worst part of it all was when she came to my house the day after she made the allegations and refused to stay around for "her" social worker to visit, I tried to stop her from leaving by holding on to her jacket and she pushed me over, leaving me on the floor, running away to her dad's without looking back to see if I was ok. I caught my hand somehow and it was bleeding, I was crying and shouting for her to help me back up as my legs had given up on me. I eventually had to call my dad to come along and help me up. My daughter now says she did not push me over or tell lies to social services. Her dad also allows her to do things that I do not approve of and I suppose as a teenager it is more attractive to be there and to be allowed to do these things but it was not what I wanted for my daughter or my son. My daughter demanded everything that belonged to her from her bedroom, so Marianne and I literally gave her everything apart from her furniture; we placed it all within large bags and left it outside the back door, inside the garden gate. The same as I did for my son, again it was a sunny day. They came and took her bags and I then went to the bathroom; I thought Marianne was joking when she shouted upstairs to tell me that my daughter, my son and their dad were bringing it all back into the garden, they were all smugly grinning. Someone had written on the two bags that they brought back 'your rubbish' (with one b) and 'you are taking the piss. I stayed inside and kept the door locked. When they had left Marianne and I took the two bags to the local dump. I got many nasty texts from her step mum, threats from her dad and ignored from my own daughter.

I get occasional visits from her but I also hope that like her brother she will realise what is right and what is wrong when she grows up and realises that her mum wanted nothing but the best for them both. It is called unconditional mothers love. I still feel that both of my kids suffered greatly before and through the messy divorce and by their dad wanting one and not the other, it was difficult enough as an adult to get through never mind a child. There are two sides to every story and I accept any blame for upsetting the kids during the break up and divorce but I will never ever forgive my ex husband for turning my kids against me and telling them lies to make himself look good.

I do feel though that when she does visits it is great and we get on, go on shopping trips or to the cinema for days out and then it feels as if it is two steps back when she does not visit or even text for weeks, it makes me feel like a fool. The last visit

I was determined that I would tell her exactly how I felt about her infrequent visits and I did, she did not take it very well, she insisted that she did nothing wrong at all and ended up storming out of the house. I told her the truth and it had to be said, she cannot be allowed to think that she can use my side of the family when it suits her then ignore us when she has what she wants, she did and said some very hurtful things to me and turned her back on her grandparents after they spoiled her rotten. This also applies to her brother but as I do not see him I cannot tell him but I would if I get the chance. They have short memories, the trips out, weekends at the cabin, presents not just on birthdays or Christmas, theatre and pantomime treats, holidays to London, Dominican Republic, various places in Scotland and my daughter went on a Mediterranean cruise with her grandparents and also for a long weekend to Blackpool with a friend, she had a limo hired for her birthday one year by my parents and my son talked my dad in to buying a dagger and two swords, all expensive and authentic, when he was going through his hunting phase, when he and my dad would go walking around the local woods. They could have been arrested if they were caught with those weapons.

21

another stepping stone

It was at this time I found that I was unable to continue with my nursery nurse role due to my MS, stress is a big factor in Multiple Sclerosis relapses and with my daughter leaving the way she did it did not help me but the worse thing happened, my mum was diagnosed with cervical cancer. I had to go off sick thinking I was relapsing as I was tiring very quickly, in pain and very slow mobility wise, which is not ideal when you have around thirty children to look after in the morning session and thirty in the afternoon session between three adults. I could not catch the little monkeys! I was off sick for around six months before I told the company that I could not continue with my employment. I say now that it was not a relapse that happened back then but reality as my mobility has not changed for the better or worse since then. I can still get around and do things that I want to do, I can drive on good days, I may get tired quickly doing simple tasks where I did not before and I get frustrated but I am determined not to let the fact that I have MS destroy my life, there are people who are not as fit as I am and they get on with life as best as they can. I manage to go shopping by myself, I can lift my wheelchair in and out of the car, push myself around the shops, I still live independently with some help from my auntie and my dad.

A year after my last full time day within the nursery I think that my life just clicked into place when I met a lovely lady called Amanda, who helps individuals who have disability issues and want to get back into the workplace. I did not feel at that time that I was confident enough to apply for another job so she asked me if I would consider volunteer within her young adults group, ages from sixteen – twenty two years, all of the individuals have a variety of disabilities or issues. My first instinct was to say no as I was used to working with under fives, it was a scary thought and I did not feel very confident at that time but I did agree to give it a go and have enjoyed every minute of it since. I am hoping that it could lead to a few paid hours but if not then I will still continue volunteering. At the moment I volunteer two days a week, on a Monday I assist a young lady with reception and cashier duties, just to boost her confidence and on a Tuesday we have our group work with the young adults, helping them get their CV's ready and helping them to apply for jobs. It can be sad when they leave to start a job or college but it can also be happy, as you feel proud that they have come on so far. I cannot help myself from get attached to them all, as I also did with the nursery children. It is also helped me with my confidence and every time I have been at the centre I come home with that 'feel good factor', when you know you have made a difference to someone's life. I have made lots of new friends and I will continue to go for as long as I am needed. The staff and young adults accept me for me and in fact one of the other volunteers, Freya said to me that I do not mention my MS at all, I just get on with things. I have only known Freya for a few months but we both feel like we have been friends for years, which is nice. If I need my wheelchair instead of my crutches I use it, I do not worry about it, I feel comfortable within the group and I never thought I would enjoy it as much as I do. It just shows you that you need to give anything a try. Life is not a rehearsal and is far too short not to at least try to do something. In fact we have done a few short plays in front of a full audience, we were all very nervous but afterwards we were all bouncing with pride and confidence. The young adults have practiced giving presentations as part of the interview process and it made me think of myself when they were asked if there was a song that best described them. Mines would need to be 'Im a Different Person' or 'Lola's Theme' by the Shapeshifters. I certainly feel like a different person, I have overcome so much and I am so proud of myself. I think about a lot; if I did not marry arse, had my two kids, gotten divorced, been diagnosed with MS then I would not be where I am now and with so many good friends around me. I feel lucky in a way. Everything happens for a reason. Ive stepped over those stones and made the most of where it took me.

I had another notion for a tattoo and I thought that because my feet were numb most of the time that I would get a sun on my right foot and a moon on my left foot. I have a thing about odd numbers so I though that it would be best that I got two done at the same time. The only problem was that as it turned out, my feet were not numb underneath the top layer of skin, I could not keep my feet still, they kept jumping. There was nothing that I could do; even Marianne tried to lean heavily on my knee to stop the jumping. The girl that does all my tattoo's ended up so frustrated that she told me to go home, this was after about two hours of foot jumping though and after we had decided that I should get some anaesthetic cream for the next time I went. The cream really worked, my foot only started to jump ten minutes before I was finished. They look good, I love them but Shelly, the tattooist says that the moon one is the worst tattoo she has ever done.

22

tiger shopping

Marianne and I have many days where we have some retail therapy; we have a coffee, some cake and hit the shops. We laugh about needing to take our big purses, in fact I thought that I would be needed my big purse one day at the local shopping centre when we stopped to admired a huge stuffed tiger in the window of one of the out of the ordinary furnishing shops, the next time we went to look in the window it was not there, I was gutted until Marianne saw that it have been moved to the back of the shop. I thought someone had bought it. Not only was it still there, it was now less than half price. No big purse required! I just had to get it, it was fate. When it was delivered the following day I was on the phone to Caroline; squealing like a dolphin about my tiger getting taken out of a van, I am surprised she made out a word I said. My neighbour was sitting on his back door step, he thought the black transit van meant that someone had died and was being removed from a house, when he saw the tiger he nearly wet himself. Not only is it six and a half foot from its nose to the end of its tail it also has a button on top of its head, when it is pressed it roars twice. I LOVE IT! I bought two big thick dog collars; I had to join them together for it to wear. I have it sitting right at my front door. My guard tiger! The local kids and also the dog walkers have a look in when they pass. My neighbours must think that I am a bit mad but I do not care a bit. Marianne and I have had many bargains at the shops but I think that was the best one to date but you never knows, as it does not take much to persuade us to go shopping.

23

the saddest day ever

The worst day of my life was the 15th of June 2011. My brave, strong and beautiful mum passed away after a very short battle against cervical cancer, she had just turned sixty-five, no age at all. We held her funeral exactly twenty-two weeks after she was first diagnosed; dad made sure she had the send off that she deserved. It just did not make sense, she never even swore and she took brilliant care of all the family. God sure does work in mysterious ways! I do not want to talk about her passing, that is personal and between mum and her family but we were all there for her at the end. I did make sure that I had time alone with her before the end to say everything that I wanted to, mainly what a great mum and gran she was and how much I loved her. John advised me to do this as when he lost his own mum he did not get the chance to do this, I am so glad that I took his advise.

I wrote her a couple of letters and put a small photo album of us all in beside her when we went to say goodbye at the funeral parlour. Her funeral was tough, I have never cried as much but I was determined to take a cord at the graveside and with a little help from my uncle I managed it, daily life is just not the same without her and I would not faint or be surprised if I went in to my dad's house and she was sitting on the couch, in her usual seat watching the television. I am told that it takes time but to be honest I know that I will not have a day without wishing that she was with us again, I would do anything, even swap her. One night I had a dream that she could come back one weekend every month, if only that could really happen. I do feel her around me at times and I believe that her spirit is with us and always will be.

Good people die young and bad people live long.

Some people change your life by coming into it and others change it by leaving.

My mum's favourite flowers were yellow roses so I got a yellow rose with mum written underneath it tattooed on to my left ankle. It is the only tattoo that my dad has not given me a telling off for; he usually says that I could get a job with the circus.

I have a memory box in my bedroom where I have kept all the of the sympathy cards I received at the time, a bottle of my mum's perfume and a few other items that belonged to her. I sometimes just lift the lid to catch a smell of her perfume when I am needing to be close to her, I miss her daily. I have found though that I can be doing something mundane in the house and I can smell her perfume, just out of nowhere, it is a comfort to me, as I believe it is her way of showing me she is still close to me. It must have been a very upsetting day for my dad when he went through my mum's jewellery boxes and gave it mostly to Andrew, Lyndsay and I; he kept a few items for himself, in fact he got her wedding ring adjusted so that he could wear it on his pinkie finger next to his own wedding ring. They were so close, never apart, he is lost without her and it kills me watching him knowing that I cant help him. I love wearing her earrings, rings or pendants, it is another way of feeling close to her. I sometimes just open one of her jewellery boxes that dad gave me, just to look or to run my finger over her things and remember when she wore them.

As a tribute to my mum we went to see 'We Will Rock You' again, it was our first Christmas without her. She loved that musical and had seen it four times already, we had all went as a family the Christmas before she passed away. The minute that the music started I could not help myself from crying and my auntie was the same, we cried all the way through it, especially when they sang the song that we had played at her funeral.

We were all wishing my mum was with us, enjoying the music again. I do not know how my dad managed to hold himself together that evening. That first Christmas and New Year was awful, like a gapping wound without her, and then we had to have her birthday without her and the first anniversary of her passing. Every month on the fifteenth dad, Lyndsay and I go up to her grave with flowers, we visit often, and dad visits twice a day. I was so proud of my dad for going back to the cabin around a month after mum passing away, to be honest with you I thought that he would give it up. It gives him somewhere to go with his wee dog, they enjoy the walks along the Loch and he always finds odd jobs to do when he is there.

Cancer Research UK holds a Race for Life annually to raise funds; Jill started participating in 2007 because of her own history and also her family's history with cancer. In 2011, Jill asked if she could add my mums name on her list of people that she was running the race for. I was so touched by this kind thought. I had a good cry.

Both my kids visited their gran in the hospital and attended the funeral; my daughter went to see her at the funeral home and wrote her a letter. Both my dad and I spoke to them at the hospital and said that life is too short to hold grudges and that their gran would want everyone in the family to stick together, we all had a cry and a hug, agreeing but unfortunately I have seen my son twice since and my daughter stopped visiting after Christmas Day. It is very sad and it hurts like hell, especially the fact that they have stopped visiting or even texting their granda that hurts me more as he needs us all around him at the moment. They have short memories of how well they were looked after before they went to live with their dad. I can only hope that when they grow up they will see sense and realise how lucky they were, let's hope they do not leave it too late. I have keepsakes in separate boxes for them for when they are older, simple things like school reports, paintings they did when they were at nursery, their first pair of shoes and the outfit that they wore home from the hospital after they were born.

24

button

I had my beautiful black cat Button since she was a kitten, nearly nine years. I had spoiled her rotten, she had a sparkly collar, tons of toys and her own cushions. Whenever she was ill I stayed up all through the night to look after her. A terrible event occurred, Button had come inside and was laying underneath my bed crying. I managed, eventually to get her out from underneath the bed and the minute I got her in to my arms I noticed that she had a stick protruding from her side, no wonder she was crying. My daughter panicked and could not help me get the stick out so I asked her to go around to my neighbours, he came around and together we got the stick out of Button and I took her straight to the vets. They advised me that this had been done deliberately and that she would be ok eventually; that in the long run it was a good thing for her to have been neutered as a kitten as this meant that she did not have any internal organs that would have been damaged by the stick. Some sick bastard had pushed a stick up inside her with such a force that it came through her side. I just hope she scratched that nasty individual to bits. The vet cleaned her up, gave her medication and told me that she just needed to be taken home to rest and recover. I stayed up all night with her to give her more medication and also to keep an eye on her, I was worried sick. She was so hot and she was crying in her sleep. I tried to keep her inside the house that night, I bought a litter tray and encouraged her to use it when she woke in the morning but she became very distressed so I had to let her out of the back door, she was always an outdoor cat anyway. I could not believe it when she jumped up and over the six-foot fence, she was obviously feeling a lot better. By the time that it took for her fur to grown back in she was back to full fitness. Thank goodness, my furry baby was ok.

It was becoming a struggle to look after Button by this time as my MS had become worse. I was not able to get down the stairs to feed her when she was hungry, I had accidentally stood on her, fell over her and could not catch the 'presents' (mice and birds) that she brought me so after many months of thinking about it I finally decided to ask the Cat Protection League if they could re-home her. I was in bits taking her to the man's house, I felt like the worst person ever, but they said that I was doing what was best for her and that they would definitely find her a good home. I received a lovely email from them around three weeks afterwards telling me that an elderly couple came in to the shelter and fell in love with her on sight, their cat had recently passed away. They took all the toys I had left, food, treats, and her likes/dislikes information that I had written down and they took Button back to their home. The Cat Protection League will keep me updated as much as they can. I still miss her but I know that it was for the best.

25

egypt

I met my friend Shannon when she started at my school in primary five after she moved into the area when her parent had separated. You would not believe how quiet she was in primary school compared to now. We had many laughs during our high school years; it is no surprise that we failed our biology exam. We chatted all the way through the class and thought that the teacher was a bit of a pervert as he would offer to check the girls in the class's necks to see if they had swollen glands if they said they were unwell. We kept in touch when she trained as a chef after we left the school. She travelled the world, working in different locations, she was even my bridesmaid when I married arse. We now live at the opposite ends of the UK but we sill keep in touch by telephone, text, or Facebook. At the beginning of this year she called me and asked me if I wanted to go abroad with her for a week to Egypt. She runs her own catering company now and could not take two weeks off, plus she said it would cheer me up after giving Button up for adoption. My initial reaction was no, I was scared as I had not been anywhere since the MS diagnosis, I asked my dad for his opinion and he said I should go for it as life is far too short, so I immediately called Shannon back and told her yes, I would love to go and I am so glad I did, we had a wonderful time in Egypt. Shannon made sure everything was taken care of so that I did not need to worry about my disability; I was extremely gratefully that she had done all of this, she really looked after me. At the airport she had arranged wheelchair assistance both at home and in Egypt, she ensured that we always got on to the plane first and when we got to the hotel in Egypt, Shannon was adamant that I wait in reception while she went with the receptionist to check that the room had a walk in shower, just as she had requested. When she came back she explained that the room that we had been allocated was too far away for me to walk to and from the pool, reception, bar and restaurants.. We got a room much closer to the all of these areas, in fact we just had to come out of the patio doors and we were a minutes walk away, the only problems was that it had only the one king size bed and that Shannon would need to sleep on a fold up bed. I told her not to bother, we could share the bed. We did this and I am glad, as I did not want Shannon to spend a week sleeping on an uncomfortable bed. We had a relaxing week in the sun, a perfect holiday. We asked at reception if we could borrow one of their wheelchairs, even just for an hour so that we could go out of the complex and see the sights but they only had two wheelchairs and they were both in use. We asked the holiday rep if he could ask one of the women who had borrowed a wheelchair if we could have it for an hour but the woman said no. I think Shannon wanted to tip her in to the pool after she said that, she had a sore foot and I am sure that she could have lent the wheelchair to us for an hour. Shannon went out and had a look around on her own, she is frightened from nothing but then she has travelled abroad on her own before. I even had a few gin's and sang karaoke twice, we also had a pamper day, sauna, massage, pedicure, manicure, steam room, a body scrub and wrap.

We enjoyed our pamper day but we could not stop laughing about how old we felt when we saw the young man who was to pamper us. He looked about fourteen years old, I could not believe it when he had finished my massage and he told me to feel his t-shirt, he asked me 'does it feel like boyfriend material'. Good grief, I had t-shirts older than him at home, I just smiled and laughed. We came back with a tan as it was roasting, in fact we got burnt, the usual for Scottish people! The mosquitoes loved to eat me but they did not touch Shannon, she found this hilarious but I was covered in bites and not laughing. I did try the swimming pool but it felt strange, like only my right leg worked and I could not even feel my MS left leg so I just lazed in the sun for the rest of the time, while Shannon went on the flumes and did the water aerobics. I was sunbathing when she came back after her attempt at the surf simulator, she could hardly tell me what happened for laughing. Eventually I got the story out of her, she told me that she lost her balance and fell off the surfboard, she lost her bikini bottoms in the fast moving water and flashed her backside to everyone who was waiting for their turn, including young children. The story got worse when she told me that the speed of the water spun her around and turned her over so not only had she given all the other hotel guests a good view of her backside she also flashed her front to them too.

When she eventually stopped and got back in to her bikini bottoms the staff member who was manning that activity laughed and said 'that happens to all the girls wearing bikinis'. The next that time she went on the surf simulator she wore her shorts! She was determined that she would manage to stay upright and she did. If it had been me, I would have stayed away after flashing my all to everyone. I can imagine that the staff member enjoys his job!

One of the waiters chatted me up every night; I hardly got peace to eat my meal. He even proposed to me! No thank you, been there, done that and do not want the t shirt, thank you. Shannon got chatting to a couple on the plane over to Egypt, the woman was also disabled and Shannon asked her what had happened to her. It turned out that she was severely disabled due to cleaning her toilet with a caustic liquid that her employer had given to her. Both her and her husband were hotel entertainers; they stayed in staff accommodation while they did this job, when she complained about the state of their bathroom she was handed a bottle of cleaner. Even although she wore gloves while she used this liquid to clean the bathroom it seeped through them and as a result she now has nerve damage, she cannot walk and will gradually get worse, including organ damage and eventually die. What a terrible story.

Now I am not as scared about travelling as I once was. In fact I have since had a weekend away with my dad, sister and brother in law to Aviemore. Mad Scottish tourists up the Cairngorms, frozen but laughing. We have had a few weekends down in Yorkshire with the relatives, feeding our faces and catching up with their news. They have been up to Scotland several times too. We have been to Eastern Europe twice so far. It is a case of 'have passport will travel' now!

26

family

I see my dad daily, he comes along and helps me with anything he can, he collects my medications for me, posts letters and puts things in the rubbish bins outside as I find it difficult to get to my bins without stumbling. My auntie Pauline comes and does my cleaning every Saturday, which I am so grateful for as all I can manage to do are my dishes, washing and ironing. I get my groceries delivered and I am lucky to have very good neighbours who put my rubbish bins out and bring them back in for me. We still have our family nights on a Thursday at dads, taking turns in who cooks the dinner, even dad cooks. I think we are trying and succeeding in doing mum proud, keeping us all together as a family, we all have our good days and bad but we know she is still with us or watching us, she is still the boss. We go out for meals more now too, on birthdays and special occasions and we also go to theatre shows, we make the most of having the family that we have. Mum would not have wanted the family to drift apart and she would not be pleased if we were all sitting miserable. Like all families we have our moments but I would say that we are pretty close. Closer now that we know someone can be taken away from you in the blink of an eye.

Dad and I have both been to see mediums regarding mum. I just wanted reassured that she passed quickly and safely, that she heard what I said and was not in any pain. I definitely got something out of it and I think my dad now believes in something he thought was rubbish previously. The medium that I have had visit my house twice already has just been and done readings for my friend Marianne, my other friend and fellow volunteer Freya, my sister and also my dad this recent month. Marta saw the ladies all in the one evening for readings, Marianne and Freya had not met before and Marianne thought that Freya was very glamorous looking; which she is, not over the top glamorous but she always looks good. I just see her as my friend who I get on very well with. Freya went first on this occasion while Marianne and I sat in my room to give them privacy, Freya's reading lasted nearly two hours then it was Marianne's turn. Freya had to get back home so I sat in my bedroom reading my latest book until Marianne's reading was over. After Marianne had left to go to her boyfriend's house it was then my turn. Marta immediately told me that my mum was with us in the lounge, that was a comfort to me. Marta got me to select a bundle of her tarot cards and through this I was told that there would be many different changes happening soon in my life and that I was not to worry about my MS getting any worse as my mum was telling her that she had a doctor with her and he was saying that as long as I remained stress free then I would stay the same as I am just now but if I let myself get stressed out then I would spend the rest of my days in a wheelchair. That would be my worst nightmare. My cards also said that the man of my dreams is just around the corner, I have not met him yet and I will not as I need to let go of John before this man would present himself to me, he would treat me well and I would have the world at my feet. BUT if I thought that John was the man that was meant for me then this man would take another path. It was my decision. Marta also told me that I should continue to keep writing as someone out there wants to read what I have to say. When she gives a reading, Marta records it on to a compact disc through her laptop and the person getting the reading done gets the disc to keep and to listen to again. I need to do this soon as I have forgotten a lot of the things that she had said to me. I was really glad that my mum came through again to tell me that she was happy where she was now and that she had the family that have passed over around her. Mum told Marta to tell my sister that she would give her a sign soon to prove that she was still with her and that she was excited about going to Disney Land in Paris with my sister and her husband at the end of next month.

I arranged for Marta to come and do a reading for my dad the following week, it is heartbreaking to see him so sad and upset when I can do nothing to help him. Dad asked me to sit in with him during his reading, I think he was a bit apprehensive as he had never met Marta or had a medium give him a reading. We sat at the dining table in the lounge and dad selected his tarot cards, when the reading began my dad's little dog started to play up, he was unsettled but Marta said that he was acting normally as animals can see people who are still alive and also spirits when they come through. When the dog went and lay down Marta said it was because my mum had told him to behave. Dad's reading lasted for over two hours, mum came through Marta to speak to my dad, she told him that he was to slow down as she feels that he does too much, especially the housework, she wants the house to look lived in and he was to stop tidying it up as much. It was very emotional but also very settling as I think that my dad felt a bit more at ease about where my mum was, she was not in the cemetery, but always by his side. She told him that she was next to him at the baby's baptism in Eastern Europe and watched him dancing while she held the baby. Marta said that my mum had another two women on either side of her and after describing them to us we both realised that it was my mum's mum and my dad's mum; both of my granny's. My dad got upset when he talked about his own mum it made me realise then that the way I was feeling about losing my mum was how he had felt, it just clicked in my head that my dad has been through what I have. My dad told Marta that he did not disbelieve in spirits and another world but he needed my mum to prove to him that she was around him. Mum told Marta that she would give him a sign but it would be when he least expected it and he was not to be hanging about waiting for it. I am not sure if my dad has listened to his recording on the compact disc yet but he can do this when he feels emotionally ready to do so. Mum also told us about how happy it made her feel when we had put a small photo album, letters, her mobile phone and other items inside her casket. Mum loved to text us all, now dad does it where he never did before. Marta ended the reading by telling him that mum like the fact that he has lots of her photo's around the house and she also said that if the dog started to play up it meant that my mum was with him. As usual Marta gave us a hug and she told my dad that he could contact her anytime he wanted if he ever needed a chat and she would come back out to see him again next year.

The extended family in Yorkshire still keep in touch, visiting and having weekends together. In fact we are due to go and visit them at the end of this month. We also try to meet up as often as possible with two of my mum's closest friends, Eve and Janette, it is so nice as they were really close to my mum and like aunties to us.

27

eastern europe

The company my brother still works for closed the factory in Livingston, where he had been working for years; he was the only employee who was transferred to their head office in London, he stayed there for around a year. Then he was asked if he would go and manage the factory in Eastern Europe for a few years. I bet he is glad that he said yes as he met and got engaged to a lovely Eastern European girl (she proposed to him on the leap year day) and his fiancé had his baby daughter at the end of May this year, just after my brother turned forty five. I think that my mum had something to do with the unexpected baby. Because my mum was not with us I felt that it was my duty to knit for the baby, they knew she was a little girl half way through the pregnancy; so I rushed out and went crazy with the pink wool. I did not know that she would not need half of the stuff that I had knitted as I had never been to Eastern Europe and my brother did not tell me that it is really warm during the summer. They have a proper summer but also have winters like Scotland does too. The family all went out to meet the new baby in the middle of June and spent a lovely relaxing week with them in a gorgeous villa. It was so warm, that the baby only needed her nappy and her vest on, we took turns at walking her while she slept in her buggy as she was more peaceful when she was on the move, she would wake up if we stopped; physio therapy for dad and myself. My brother did most of the cooking when we ate in the villa, he would tell you to get out of the kitchen if he was a bit grumpy, I stayed clear as I have lived and also worked with him; I know how grumpy he can be. We had meals out and dad even tried the traditional Eastern European Chorba soup. Which is brave of him as he is such a fussy eater, he mainly sticks to plain dishes.

On the fifth of August we all went back for a long weekend where they had their baby girl baptised, it is a big deal over there, extremely religious ceremony, huge meal afterwards, flowers and favours for the guests. It was brilliant to see my dad smiling and dancing; enjoying himself, almost like his old self. The next morning he wondered why his knees were so painful, it had been years since he had been up dancing all night at a party. We were all still grieving for mum but we all made sure that we enjoyed the day and the party because we had my brother's new baby to celebrate. The only bad thing about that weekend is that the mosquitoes munched away at my legs again and that I had a very bad fall and split my eyebrow open, I think I am going to be left with a lovely scar. I was sharing a room with my dad when we were over, I got up to use the bathroom in the early hours, feeling unsteady; when I stumbled I did not want to fall on top of my dad's bed and wake him up so I stumbled the other way and hit my face right on the corner edge of the wall, I did not realise how bad it was until I got in to the bathroom and noticed that my pyjamas were covered in blood. I knew that it was a sore bump but I thought that I would just have a small bruise. It is the worst stumble I have had to date. The next time I am going to wake him, it wont hurt as much. Well, not for me anyway! Oh well, it is a reminder of the weekend when my first niece got baptised.

I must be driving my friends insane, as every time my brother sends new photos of the baby I pass them on by email, I cannot help it; I am an auntie for the very first time and very excited about it. My brother and his family will be coming to Scotland to spend Christmas and New Year with us, the baby will have changed so much by then. I cannot wait to see her, I was crying at the airport saying goodbye to her after the baptism weekend. We keep in touch with them by Skype, it is not the same as being in the same room as them but technology is great! Dad would like to have a celebration in her honour and I have started to organise this for him in the church where her daddy, both of her aunties were Christened and where her Scottish grand parents were married; this will take place between Christmas and New Year, the baby will wear the family Christening robe that her daddy and her aunties have worn before her. My own daughter also had it on at her Christening.

Dad will throw her a big family party; he is really looking forward to it. No doubt he will be dancing the night away again and end up with sore knees the next day. There will be a large cake and we will have a meal, it is exciting and it gives us all something to look forward to, as we will be sad that it is another Christmas and New Year without our mum. I just have to order the invitations and that will be it all sorted!

28

life now

One perk of having MS is the mobility car; I was financially able at the time to put money towards the advanced payment and I got a BMW 1 series coupe sport in Sorrento red. When I had it for just a fortnight, I was sitting at a roundabout waiting for my turn to go and a young girl bashed into the back of me, I was gutted but the insurance sorted it out. I am glad they did as the girl's father called me and was abusive over the phone. When the garage came to take the car away to be repaired I nearly cried until the courtesy car arrived, an Audi TT. I 'enjoyed' having that car for the week it took to repair my BMW. I managed to 'push' the TT to do 126 miles per hour. I love my posh BMW, at the moment I have had it two years and next year I plan to get myself a Mini Countryman, room for my wheelchair (that I occasionally use now) and I definitely need to get an automatic. I also have a blue badge, which means that I can park closer to the shops or other different places, privileged parking!

I know that my MS has become slightly worse since my diagnosis, I walk with a slight limp, my whole left side has less power than the right, even typing this I have trouble with the left hand side of the keyboard as I do not have as much power in my left hand as I do in my right. After my holiday in Egypt I have managed to lose two and a half stone in weight, which now I feel better for and I think that it is better for my body too as my legs do not have to carry as much weight as they used to. On a good day I use a stick to assist me with my balance and on bad days I use an arm crutch, on very bad days it is the wheelchair's turn. Along with my stair lift and my wet floor shower room, I also have a shower chair just outside the cubicle that I have only used a few times, there is a frame around my toilet so that I can get up and down easier. I have a chair in the kitchen so I can sit while the kettle boils or when I am making meals, I have a walking stick at the top of my stairs just in case I need to use it, I had to get a higher king size divan bed as the bed I had was far too low for me to get up and out of. I could have ended up rocking myself back to sleep when I was trying to get up and out of my old bed! All the things I never wanted and said I would not use, but I do without thinking about it now. I said previously that all these things were for grannies; now I realise they are designed to help 'anyone' and to make life easier and safer. I have covered my stair lift and my wheelchair with stickers, I bought my stick specifically because it is the same colour as my car. I do not do boring! Having MS does not change the fact that I am still myself, it just makes me a bit different and it is good to be different at times. I am a very determined person and I will not let it get the better of me, I do have my good days where I may be slow but still manage and I will have my bad days where I will struggle, get frustrated and have a good bloody cry. I am much stronger than I thought I ever was before. I have coped with a sham of a marriage, a messy nasty divorce, my kids leaving my house and having no contact with them, threats from my ex husband and his new wife, who has now left him!! My mum passing away was dreadful, having a debilitating condition and yet I still can laugh and see the good side in things and in people.

Even on days when I am exhausted due to my condition I find it hard to sit still, I cannot rest; it is just not me. I am an on the go sort of person and this is why I can get so frustrated when I am unable to do the things that I want to. I admit that I do have a 'slight' obsessive-compulsive disorder, OCD's. I must have things in a certain order, my blinds must be sitting correctly, the coasters on my coffee table must match and be in line with each other and my towels must be hung over the towel rail in a straight line. I just like things to look neat, there is nothing wrong with that! I really dislike when I see an electrical socket that is switched on but has no plug in it, I have to switch it off as it just is not right. However, I am not as compulsive as I used to be because I began to notice that when my son was small he would copy me in straightening up the back door mat or the DVD's on the shelf. I did not want him to grown up with OCD's. My pet hate is people who are noisy eaters, there is no need to eat with your mouth open. Manners cost nothing. It nearly makes my teeth bleed!

I am not able to donate blood now, I have only done it three times before anyway so that was not a huge blow; I need all my blood for myself. The MS experts do not know if I would be able to donate my organs, I have been told that it would be the decision of the recipient whether they were willing to take the risk of getting MS as well as a new organ. The amount of pills I have to take on a daily basis may also be another reason for me not being able to donate my blood or my organs. I take over ten different types of medication in pill form every day, my chemist has them set up in a dosette packet, which has them in different sections for morning, mid morning, evening and night time. This is additional to my injections that I must do every other day and the pain relief I take if and when I need it. MS can cause confusion and memory loss; I seem to be ok as far as this is concerned at the moment, lets hope that it continues. The only side effect that I have experience with this new DMD's is that on the nights when I have had my injection I have very strange dreams. I dreamt about my sister having three piglets as well as her three little dogs, how they were running around our granda's roses and he was shouting at them, in another dream my sister had a little boy of around two and none of the family knew about him. There are also scary dreams or nightmares where I am still living with arse and he is being nasty to me; I have also had a nightmare where an intruder had broken in to my house and raped me. I could do nothing to fight him off due to my MS, as my lack of strength was much worse in this dream. It is a pity that I cannot choose to just have good dreams instead of nightmares.

I have moments where I wonder if I can still do things that I used to do, I got it in to my head that I wanted to attempt running, just to see if I still could. I made sure that I was safe, I had the wall on one side and the stair banister on the other, not only did I try and fail once but I tried it again (just to make sure) and failed, so I guess that I cannot run like I used to but at least I tried it. My running is not pretty or fast, in fact I would not call it running at all. I have ideas about activities that I want to try like attempt the climbing wall at the nearby indoor rock-climbing centre. I do still enjoy sketching; in fact I have many of my sketches framed and up on my walls. I also have one of my daughter's sketches up on my kitchen wall and I have seen how well my son can sketch; I must have passed on this talent to them both as my paternal granda passed it on to me, through my mum. My auntie Pauline asked me to do four sketches that she could give her friends for their Christmas gifts and Marianne also found a picture of her mum's favourite flowers, iris's, and she asked me to sketch it for her mum's Christmas, she was so pleased with it that she has it on her lounge wall. I am quite gifted with craft things; I have made a small kilt for a teddy that Marianne has in her car; it was designed to cover his 'modesty' as he usually only wore his his Y front underpants. One of Marianne's hobbies is collecting doll's houses and the furniture to match them, she asked me to re-cover the lounge sofa that she had in one of her houses to match a new theme that she was doing. I did this for her over one weekend, all my stitching is done by hand; I do not own a sewing machine. I really take pleasure in doing my craft activities and I enjoy looking at the finished product; the delight on the face of the person who asked me to do the job when I have finished is so satisfying. I still continue knitting, ive knitted jumpers for babies abroad for charities.

This year the nasty cancer disease took Caroline's mum; another good person that did not deserve it. Dad and I attended her funeral along with Janette, her husband Grant and Eve. It was very sad and brought back to me the fact that I had lost my own mum and also to my dad that his wife was gone. It was the first funeral he had attended since mum had passed away; he was extremely brave. It was my third as I had previously accompanied Pauline to her uncle's and then to her auntie's funeral; I went in my mum's place.

I am sure I have a long road left. Lets hope karma is on my side because it is definitely my turn to be dealt a good hand, until then I will just keep taking my pills and injection; continuing to just being me and smile and laugh. I am willing to try anything that may improve my MS, I take vitamin D, and I have a small labradorite stone beside my bed as I had read that it has the power to speed up healing. The local gym has a machine called a Power Plate, which I have used; it can build up your core strength as well as tone your muscles. I went weekly until last year when I thought I was having a relapse and when my mum was going through her treatment before she passed away. I did not have the energy or the inclination then but I will get back in to it soon, as I found that it helped me, the good thing is that the gym manager also has MS so she understands how I feel.

All I would like in my future is to be happy, to smile daily, a cure for MS would be good too and maybe I will find my ideal man who will treat me the same way as my dad treated my mum. A girl can dream!

Watch this space, as you never know what is around the corner. I live everyday, as if it could be my last. I have learnt the hard way that life is much too short and it is not a rehearsal. Try everything at least once and have no regrets because you cannot press the rewind button in life. Stay calm and take the stepping stones slowly to reach your dreams.

A wise woman once told me that 'You are only dealt a hand that you can cope with; then it is up to you how you play the game of life'

www.ingramcontent.com/pod-product-compliance
Lightning Source LLC
Chambersburg PA
CBHW020423290526
45785CB00002B/703